Samuel MacNaughton

Lily and Leander

The Secret of Success in Service

Samuel MacNaughton

Lily and Leander
The Secret of Success in Service

ISBN/EAN: 9783744776387

Printed in Europe, USA, Canada, Australia, Japan

Cover: Foto ©Thomas Meinert / pixelio.de

More available books at **www.hansebooks.com**

LILY AND LEANDER;

OR,

THE SECRET OF SUCCESS IN SERVICE:

A Poem of Life,

AND OTHER

POEMS AND HYMNS.

BY THE

Rev. SAMUEL MACNAUGHTON, M.A.,

AUTHOR OF "THE GOSPEL IN GREAT BRITAIN;" "JOY IN JESUS: MEMORIALS
OF BELLA DARLING;" "DOCTRINE AND DOUBT;" "OUR CHILDREN FOR
CHRIST;" "THE WINES OF SCRIPTURE—A BIBLICAL AND HISTORICAL
INQUIRY;" "THE DUTY OF THE CHRISTIAN CHURCH IN RELATION
TO TEMPERANCE" (A PRIZE ESSAY), ETC., ETC.

EDINBURGH:

JAMES GEMMELL, 19 GEORGE IV BRIDGE.

1890.

Dedication.

— · · ·

This volume is respectfully and affectionately dedicated to the Office-Bearers and Members of the Church under my Pastoral Care, whose hearty appreciation of the high-toned spiritual teaching, which finds an echo in this work, suggested to me the expediency of recording in verse Christian Experiences, personally known to myself, in the form in which 'Lily and Leander' appears.

PREFACE.

THE Theological Novel has become a recognised factor in the religious thought of our day. The three works, bearing this character, which have recently excited attention,—'ROBERT ELSMERE,' 'JOHN WARD, PREACHER,' 'THE STORY OF AN AFRICAN FARM,'—although in some respects ably written, with powerful delineations of character, do not present an adequate view of Christianity. The writers have sought rather to caricature the Christian religion, than to give a faithful representation of it. In 'Lily and Leander' there is no attempt to reply to any of the arguments set forth in these works; but simply, under the form of a life-story, and a frank recital of difficulties and genuine experience, to illustrate various phases of the possible and actual religious life, and especially the higher and more mature experiences of FAITH, and PEACE, and POWER, and JOY in WORK, and perfect freedom from WORRY and CARE.

As stated in the DEDICATION, the idea of this work occurred to me as feasible, and as likely to be useful, by the intense earnestness and profound impression produced by the recital from the pulpit at the close of the sermon of some of the Hymns to be found in this volume,—notably, "STEP BY STEP WITH JESUS," "TO LIVE IS CHRIST," "TO DIE IS GAIN," "SOUL-LONGINGS," and "LIGHTS AND SHADOWS IN LIFE." I was thereby convinced that there was nothing equal to high-toned spiritual teaching and experience, clothed in homely language, and presented in simple verse, to arrest the ear, and touch the conscience and heart; and was thus induced to undertake this work, and to cast it into its present form.

The plan of the story will be found true to life. " Lily," gifted, earnest, enthusiastic, undertakes rough Christian work among the poor, with but few tokens of success, and attributes her failure to the natural and inherent weakness of Woman. All the while, however, she has been labouring in her own strength, and neglecting to appropriate the promises, given by Christ to all labourers in His vineyard, that He will continually guide, and strengthen, and clothe with power, those who trustfully look to Him and lean upon Him.

"Leander," who has attained a higher experience, having earlier entered into the Christ-life, leads her on, step by step, until she enters the REST OF FAITH, and rejoices in her new-found power in service. The recitals of their personal experience, as they entered upon the Higher Life of Holiness and Consecration, are not imaginary, nor are they exaggerated.

Hundreds of earnest Christians can testify that such experiences are actual facts in their own personal history; and can note with perfect clearness the different stages in their spiritual growth, as set forth in this "poem of life."

The TWENTY HYMNS on Scripture Texts and on Holiness and Consecration have been selected as being in harmony with the general purpose of the Life-Story in picturing forth the higher phases and experiences of the spiritual life. A few of them have been printed on New Year's Cards for private distribution. The hymn, "To Die is Gain," bears a resemblance to one on the same text in Dr. Grosart's noble work, "Three Centuries of Hymns," just published, in the use of the text as a refrain. In thought they are as wide as the poles asunder. Both hymns are entirely independent —both being written months before the publication of either volume, and both being in the printer's hands at the same time.

The Twenty Early Poems are selected from a considerable number published in Canadian periodicals during the author's early college days. Variety of topic was the dominant idea in making the selection.

ADDISON ROAD, PRESTON,
  NOVEMBER, 1889.

CONTENTS.

		PAGE
Dedication,	. . . . .	iii
Preface,	. . . . .	v
Contents,	. . . . .	ix
Plan of the Poem,	. . .	xi

LILY AND LEANDER :

Part I.—Service and Failure,	.	1
Part II.—Trial and Consecration,		37
Part III.—The Life of Faith,	. . .	70

HYMNS ON HOLINESS AND CONSECRATION :—

Lights and Shadows in Life,	.	109
Soul-Longings,	. . . .	115
Step by Step with Jesus,	. . . .	117
Consecration,	. . .	121
To Live is Christ,	. . .	124
To Die is Gain,	. . . . .	127
The New Name,	. . . . .	129
The Mount of Holiness,	. . .	133
Bread of Heaven,	. . . .	134
God's Leading,	. . . .	136
Jesus Only,	. . . . .	139
The Christian Life,	. . . .	141
Three Voices,	. . . .	143
Call to Consecration,	. . .	145
Consecration,	. . . . .	147

PAGE

HYMNS ON HOLINESS AND CONSECRATION :—

Shining for Christ, ... 148
New Year's Hymn, ... 150
New Year's Hymn, ... 152
New Year's Hymn, ... 154
New Year's Hymn, ... 155

EARLY POEMS :—

For an Album, ... 159
A Summer's Morn, ... 160
The Talking Zephyr, ... 162
The Two Flower Gardens, . . . 164
A Midnight Reverie, ... 166
Solitude, ... 168
Love's Token, ... 170
Forget Me Not, ... 173
Ode to Spring, ... 174
My Birthday, ... 175
The Missionary, ... 177
The Ill-fated "Atlantic," 180
My School, ... 182
The Minstrel's Fatherland, ... 186
In Memoriam—Hon. Joseph Howe, Lieutenant-
 Governor of Nova Scotia, . . . 188
In Memoriam—Thomas Morrison, . . . 191
On the Death of a Child, ... 193
Hymn on Affliction, ... 194
The Dying Year, ... 195
The Snowdrop, ... 196

LILY and Leander at the close of School-days devote themselves to Christian work. Lily, bright, brilliant, enthusiastic, panting for service, sets to work among the poor, hoping by love, tact, and enthusiasm to win men from their evil courses. She wins their praises, but not their lives; and attributes her failure to the natural weakness of woman.

Leander, who has lived on the higher platform of fellowship with Christ, points out to her that woman may be strong—in fact *is* strong in the very elements of character in which Jesus manifested strength,— in love, pity, sympathy, tenderness, gentleness. He shows her that she must walk in Christ's footsteps, and, like Paul, have "the power of Christ" resting upon her, if she would win men from evil, and lift them up to a higher and nobler life. Men, as well as women, are powerless for good without divine help and guidance.

After receiving new light Lily still feels her inability to comfort the sad and sorrowful and down-trodden on account of her inexperience of suffering. She is led to see this by the plaintive wail :—

> " You have not suffered ; have you, Miss ?
> You have not been in plight like this."

Therefore in Part II. it is shown that, if one would have abundant success in service, one must have *sympathy;* and sympathy is born of suffering. To be a universal comforter one must suffer in *body,* in *intellect,* and in *heart;* so as to be able to sympathize with all forms of suffering. Thus was Jesus tried.

To be strong for work we must be free from worry and anxious care. Hence Part III. deals with Consecration and the Rest of Faith. WILL and WORK and WAY must all be committed to God. The Life of Faith brings not only a wondrous Peace, but also new Power in service. Instead of labouring in our own strength, we let God use us, just as He pleases—how, and when, and where, and with what results,—and we are at perfect peace. And where there is NO WORRY, there is NO WEAR. This is the true secret of a happy life, and the secret also of success in service.

LILY AND LEANDER:

A POEM OF LIFE.

PART I.—SERVICE AND FAILURE.

COME, Lily, trusty friend of yore,
And let me see your treasure-store
Of loving service, since the day
We pledged ourselves to work and pray
For human weal.   The years have sped,
But I have treasured all you said:
" I would not live to win a name,
" Or climb with man the heights of fame;
" Nor would I ever rest content
" With being Fashion's ornament—
" A thing to be admired, and praised,
" And petted.   I should feel abased
" By being set in such false place,—
" 'Twere like fair cherub fall'n from grace.
" I would be loving, helpful, kind;
" My greatest joy I aye would find

A

" In doing good.   Where sin is rife,
" There I would help men in the strife :
" Would brighten their most cheerless lot,
" And make a little heaven each cot."

Leander, 'twas a girl's resolve :
I smile to think you did revolve
In your large cranium so long
My girlish words, more weak than strong.
I meant them then, for I was young :
Life's tuneless song had not been sung :
Sweet music everywhere I found ;
Enthusiasm o'erleaped all bound.
Lo ! youth is eager, hopeful, brave,
To be and do it aye doth crave.
Impulsive, moved by varying mood,
I on life's threshold panting stood.
I longed and yearned and agonized
For service—oft too lightly prized.
Let me have work, or low or high ;
To be a drone would be to die.
It seemed to be my daily food
Each fleeting day to do some good :
And, Cæsar-like, I oft would say :
" I've done no good ; I've lost a day."

But, Lily, why " no good," I pray ?
Need earnest soul e'er lose a day ?

Work done for God must aye endure ;
For still the promise standeth sure :
" He who goes forth with precious seed,—
" Lo ! weeping, hungry souls to feed,—
" His ripened sheaves shall doubtless bring,
" And grateful heart for joy shall sing."
The fruit of toil may not be seen
On day of labour ; for between
The sowing and the reaping day
The summer months have sped away.
And oft good seed has hidden lain,
Till summer sun and timely rain
Have caused the germ to sprout and spring :
In Autumn back our sheaves we bring.
And, lo ! in Nature I have found
That seed that lies long underground,
And plants that are in growth most slow,
Most fruitful are, and strongest grow.
The stately oak that braves the blast
Of storm and tempest is the last
To gain its size and giant strength.
And patient toilers find at length
That 'tis the same in realm of grace :
It is not those of quickest pace ;
Nor those who start first in the race,
Who in the end take foremost place.
The deepest waters move but slow ;
But they are strong in onward flow.

And we may find stout hearts of oak
Among unlearnèd common folk,
If we have patience with their ways,
And cheerly brook their long delays.
If you have sown good seed in May,
Pray, do not think you've lost a day,
Because you have not gathered fruit
Before the seed has taken root.
In AUTUMN look for golden grain
To gild and deck each field and plain.

Leander, were I strong, like you,
And eloquent, then I might do
Some lasting good among the poor,
And hope from sin them to allure;
But, lo! I spend my strength for naught.
By toil and counsel I have sought
To save the fallen, help the weak;
But the more earnestly I seek
To lift them up, the more I see
Of helpless, hopeless misery.
Betimes my heart is sad and crushed
By tale of woe; my voice is hushed,
As oft they tell of men for gain
Oppressing them with galling chain
Of servitude,—yea, "Christian" men,—
May I not hear such tales again!

Lo! I have thought that MEN must go
To haunts of misery, and show,
By generous deed and loving word,
That Christian hearts are deeply stirred
With sympathy for all oppressed,
And long to make their lives more blessed.
We women cannot cope with woe;
We're weak, and tears too quickly flow.

But, Lily, I would dare dispute
That weakest woman should be mute,
While her own sex needs helping hand:
She may be strong, and take her stand
With Christ and Christly men, and go
To lowest haunts of direst woe,
And rise above her tears and sighs,
And smile at toil and sacrifice,
And bring rich benison to those
Whose life is naught but throbs and throes.
Her cheery word and kindly heart,
Her skilful tact and subtle art,
Will woo and win the dullest soul, —
The sad and lone will quick console,—
If in the name of Christ she goes
To minister to human woes.

Leander, you are strong in mind,
One of the strongest of your kind;

Like lark, at morning dawn, you soar
And sing until your trouble's o'er.
You men are favoured more than we;
For woman's weak; and easily
She's overcome by pressing ills,—
Her heart with sorrow quickly fills.
Your manly eyes know naught of tears,
While woman's eyes rain forth her fears.
Why did our God thus make us weak,
That we to man for strength must seek ?—
Must cling to him in trying hour
And all our plaints upon him shower ?

But, Lily, if a man may speak,
Defending God for making weak
The gentler sex, then I make bold
To lead you back to stories told
Of Woman in the olden time,
Which seem to me not quite to chime
In with your view of your own dower,
As being scant in strength and power.

See Deborah once leading out
The hosts of God their foes to rout;
While Barak in this testing hour
Reveals the might of Woman's power.
As prophetess of God Most High
She sendeth forth the battle cry :

" Up, Barak Ben-Abinoam,
" The call to battle quick proclaim ;
" Ten thousand men are at thy call ;
" With them on Jabin's captain fall.
".Lo ! Sisera and his proud hosts stand
" On Kishon's banks.   There by thy hand,
" And in the name of God Most High,
" This very day they all must die.
" Up, play the man, be strong, be brave ;
" And from their en'mies Israel save."

Was Barak strong to do and dare ?
Or, must a woman with him share
The burdens and the spoils of war,
And ride in the triumphal car ?

" If thou with me wilt go," he said,
" Then I will go, and nothing dread ;
" But, if with me thou wilt not go,
" My back I turn upon the foe."

Was Deborah, a woman, WEAK ?
Hark ! these the words she quick did speak :
" I certainly shall go with thee ;
" But, lo ! thy fame eclipsed shall be ;
" In woman men shall make their boast
" For crushing Sisera's proud host."

Say, Lily, was this woman WEAK?
Did Fear's cold pallor tinge her cheek?

No; Deborah was brave, and strong
To help the weak, and right the wrong;
But she who won this meed of praise
Was born and reared in far-off days.
Where do we find a woman now
Of lion-heart, who will not bow
Beneath her burden and her care,
And rush to man, that he may share
Her trials, and upon him cast
Her troubles, coming thick and fast?
We're weak to-day—we women are,—
Ay, born beneath some fateful star;
We start and quiver, shriek and sigh,
And aye look forth through tear-dimmed eye.

Ah! Lily, say not you are weak;
For woman's strong, and I must speak
Of stories modern I have heard,
As whispered by some little bird.
A girl, yet in her teens, was tried,
And every artful lure defied.
A lordling, full of passion, thought
That woman's virtue could be bought.
He offered gifts and diamonds rare,
If she would but consent to share

With him in ways not good and pure;
And strove by bribes her to allure.

But was she weak? Ah! did she yield?
No, no; her virtue proved her shield.
She spurned with scorn the villain's bait,
And answered proffered love with hate.
Was she not strong? say, was she weak?
Ah! why the rose upon your cheek?
Why mantles in your face a flush,
That melts away in sweetest blush?
O can it be, sweet lily fair,
That I've unconsciously laid bare
A chapter in your own pure life
That proves you strong.
                           Ah! sin is rife:
And MEN are weak. To sin is weak.
He who by wicked arts would seek
To blast the bloom on Beauty's cheek
Has not in him the faintest streak
Of manly strength or nobleness;
He's but a brute, nor more nor less.
You who resist are strong and brave:
'Tis lives like yours the world will save.
She's strong who's pure in life and heart,
Whose shield aye saves from tempter's dart.

'Tis nothing that we should say, NO
To one we know is virtue's foe;

To woman 'tis a thing of course
To guard herself, ev'n by sheer force,
From aught that could or dim or stain
Her name,—more precious than all gain.
Mere self-defence ! an instinct found
In things that burrow underground,—
In lowest orders of the race
That run on legs, and in the chase
Do rush and hide, or run away,
That life may be prolonged a day !
THIS call not strength—mere self-defence—
Mere love of life—in all intense.
I long to see in woman MIND—
Keen intellect—a heart refined—
A mental grip and grace combined :
'Tis strength like this I long to find.

But, lo ! I see on every hand,
At home, abroad, in every land,
That woman takes inferior place,
And dares not risk to run a race
With brother-man for any prize,
That's dear in noble woman's eyes.
Is this not weak ? Leander, say,
Where are our women of to-day,
Whose power of will, whose strength of nerve,
Can win for them the right to serve

In spheres where grip and grasp of mind
Are requisites?   Ah! you are kind,—
Too kind, I ween, to our weak race,—
Enamoured aye of Beauty's face.

  But, Lily, prithee, list to me:
The strength you seek I surely see
In many of your sex to-day,
Who've nobly wrought, and won their way
To place and power in doing good,—
In patience training natures rude,—
By converse pure, and lofty life
Uplifting man above all strife
Between the passions, base and low,
And high and noble aims, that grow
More strong by keeping touch with you,
Who him baptize with heavenly dew.
Yes, woman's power is daily seen,
Like sun-lit rays of golden sheen,
In brightening man's daily toil ;
On troubled waters pouring oil ;
In rearing " rose-buds," good and pure ;
And making " olive-plants " secure
From tempter's dart and passion's snare—
Thus clothing them with beauty rare.
And woman's strength is oft displayed
In bringing crushed hearts timely aid,—

Her loving sympathy outflows
From gentle heart—a balm for woes ;
In snatching sisters, oft ingrate,
From dismal life and sadder fate.
A woman's love and gentleness ;
A woman's insight and address ;
A woman's patient, watchful care ;
A woman's pleading, tearful prayer,
Have power to win where sin is rife,—
To touch the heart and change the life :
Such power as this, to woman given,
Is richest, noblest gift of Heaven.

Say, Lily, is not woman strong,
Whose presence fills sad hearts with song ?
Whose love oft clings to broken reed
With faintest hope that she may lead
Frail man in path both safe and plain,
And bring him back to God again ?
Is she not brave, is she not strong,
Who meekly suffers daily wrong ?
Whose heart stores up the direst grief,
Refusing aye to seek relief
By telling forth a husband's sins,
And making known his outs and ins ?
Is woman weak, when suffering child
Has from her weary eye beguiled

All sleep and rest, she watches on
Through cheerless nights, her bloom all gone;
Thinks not of self, but bravely bears
With cheerful hope her load and cares?
Ah ⊦ no, she's strong and brave of heart;
In life, not man could take her part.

Leander, truly you plead well
The cause of woman; but she fell,—
Fell first before the tempter's spell,—
So men in ancient story tell.
And still she falls—is weak from birth;
And weakness seems her dower on earth.

Fell first, and farthest?   Lily, lo!
The man was weak.   This I would know:
Why did he not ward off the blow,
So subtly dealt by wily foe?
If he were strong, one would have thought
He would most eagerly have sought
To match his strength 'gainst tempter's art,
And buttress his fair partner's heart.
If strong in wisdom he could plead
That they must loathe all selfish greed;
That love to God and purity
Would aye the path of safety be;
That God was loving, wise, and just,
And they His wisdom aye must trust:

The fruit, so tempting to their eyes,
And much desired to make them wise,
Was under ban for reasons good;
For God knew what was "good for food."

The man was weak, as woman weak;
And why? Because he did not seek
The strength and fellowship of God,
But quick did yield to tempter's nod.
Good mother Eve some strength displayed;
She argued, reasoned, "God hath said,
"'On day thou eatest thou shalt die'—
"A clear command from God Most High;
"Thou shalt not eat of this one tree—
"A test of love and loyalty.
"I dare not take, as thou me bidd'st,
"Of Tree that standeth in the midst
"Of the fair Eden, nor as much
"As with my finger lightly touch."
She met the tempter—reasoned well
With the archfiend and prince of hell.
And, if the man had backed her up,
She might, in truth, the poisoned cup
In easy triumph back have hurled;
And by the act, have saved a world.
But man stood by, a weakling he,
And sinned in silence by the tree;

By silence he offended first,—
A coward!—his offence was worst.

　Leander, you much art display;
Your reasoning I can't gainsay;
'Tis new to hear the case put thus—
The Fall brought home to you, not us.
In Holy Writ do we not read
That Paul 'gainst woman seeks to plead,
That she was in transgression first;
By woman's weakness man was cursed?

　'Tis not quite thus he puts the case:
Nor gives to her precedent place.
"In the transgression," true, 'tis said:
Not "first," or deepest, as I've read.
Th' Apostle's words are very mild;
He says, "the woman was beguiled."
Not she alone received the curse
Which clearly proves she was no worse
Than lordly man in the offence,
Which shadowed mis'ries so immense.
The woman, lo! had hardest plight;
Alone the archfiend she must fight;
With wily words and subtle art,
He trapped her unsuspecting heart.
Too strong in trustfulness perchance,
She quick did yield to his advance.

But man met not the tempter's art;
His subtle words ne'er reached his heart,
And yet he fell, as quick as she,
And ate of the forbidden tree.
And, if she first did take and eat,
Perchance the man thought it was meet
That she who came as his "helpmeet,"
Should run the risk of such a feat,
And be the first to test the word
Forespoken by Elohim Lord.
His weakness made him hesitate,
And send the woman to her fate.
Lo! he was "with her" 'tis declared;
The tempting fruit *with him* she shared.
She must have had his full consent;
His silence showed his heart's intent.
No word he spoke to check rash act;
No pressure used, nor skilful tact;
No plea for God, as Father, Friend,
His wisdom seeking to commend;
No warning word 'gainst certain doom,—
That disobedience would entomb
Their noblest pleasures, richest joys,—
The gladd'ning sound of God's own voice.
If Adam had but played the man,
He might have foiled the tempter's plan;
If strong, his strength should be a shield.
Which he, if brave, could deftly wield

To drive the tempter from the field ;
But, lo ! a weakling, see him yield !
So, Lily, I would, by your leave,
Make Adam ev'n more weak than Eve.
Not weaker, nor less tried that day,
Nor first, nor deepest in the fray,
Was woman, mother of our race :
I still would give her foremost place.

Leander, I admit the force
Of all you say ; your great resource
Of argument and skilful tact
Throws brightening light on that sad fact.
If man had helped, she might have stood,
And have been surnamed Eve the Good.
But still in every age and race
The woman takes inferior place ;
She's slave to man in olden time
In every tribe, in every clime ;
And, even now, she does not rise,
With manly might, and snatch each prize
Of place and honour and renown ;
But leaves to man official gown.
In court of law no woman pleads ;
Nor hungry souls from pulpit feeds ;
In seat of Justice does not sit,
As if for such high place unfit ;

In Parliament she has no voice ;
Not ev'n of those who speak the choice :
Yet she has many wrongs to right,
And many needs to bring to light,
Of which she truly best could speak,
Were she not deemed inferior, weak.

Yes, Lily, by some strange sad freak,
Lo! Woman's *deemed* inferior, weak :
Such is the custom of our time—
A custom neighbour near to crime,—
A relic strange of barbarous age,
'Gainst which a righteous war I'd wage.
Much, very much, the world has lost,
As man is finding to his cost,
By giving woman lower place,
Excluding her from honour's race.
God made the woman from man's own
New-formèd flesh and blood and bone,
That, long as earthly cycles run,
Man might regard the woman one
With him in honour, place, and power :
To Woman this was Heaven's dower.

Man needs pure woman's gentle might ;
Man needs a woman's gladd'ning light ;
Man needs a soft, persuasive voice
To guide him and direct his choice

To noble aims, to pleasures pure,
To joys that evermore endure.
Man wants to see self-sacrifice
Each day lived out before his eyes :
He wants to see all self repressed,
The heart, meanwhile, at perfect rest :
He wants to see that gentleness
Is mightiest power he can possess.
He wants to see how kindness wins
The hardest from debasing sins.
He wants to feel the power of love
Uplifting him, like soaring dove,
To regions free from earthly taint,
Till heart becomes the heart of saint.

Leander, pray, is this all true ?
Has woman power thus to renew
The life and change the heart of man,
So wayward since the world began ?
Could I be sure such power was mine,
I never would again repine,
Or murmur that our God had made
Us women weak, as I have said.

Yes, Lily, it is all most true;
With men omnipotent are you,
When, filled with love and gentleness,
In Christly ways you seek to bless.

God's ministers you're called to be ;
And yours is noblest ministry.
Like Jesus, seeking no renown ;
Like Him, not easily cast down ;
Like Jesus, loving, gentle, kind,
In troubled hearts quick place you find.
Like Jesus, touched by human woes,
In tears your sympathy outflows :
Most mighty is the power of tears ;
For nothing human so endears.

You say you deem it weak to weep
Let the assertion have full sweep :
Then God was weak when " Jesus wept."
Are tears not treasures to be kept
And used as ministers of love,
To lift up tearful hearts above
The sorrows that have pressed them sore,
By seeing other hearts run o'er
For them in loving sympathy ?
Lo ! thus our tears may blessings be.

'Tis not for Lazarus Jesus weeps ;
For he had said, " Lo ! Lazarus sleeps:"
The sleeper He would soon awake,
And his new life more glorious make.
Nor does He for the sisters weep ;
His tryst with them He'll surely keep ;

To them their brother He'll restore,
And they shall need to weep no more.

Then why, Leander, did He weep ?
Had He some hidden purpose deep
To show that He was truly man ?
Was this in God's predestined plan ?

Now, Lily, you do talk like men,
Who sit in College chairs, and pen
Huge dissertations, learned and long,
In phrases logical and strong.
Yourself are strong, if I may speak :
A woman ! yet you are not weak.

But, why did Jesus weep, you ask ?
I turn with pleasure to the task
Of showing why the strong should weep ;
For 'tis as natural as sleep.
WITH them He weeps—He shares their tears:
By sympathy their hearts He cheers.
'Tis strong to weep as Jesus wept,—
To share tears shed for one who " slept,"—
To sympathize with troubled heart,—
To ease its pain and heal its smart.
And, Lily, you, who're strong to weep,
Rich golden sheaves of thanks should reap :
Your tenderness—your richest dower—
Aye clothing you with heavenly power.

These, then, prime elements of strength,
At which we have arrived at length :
Not strength of muscle or of brain
A prize to win, quick lost again,
When stronger hand, or richer mind,
Ambitious, presses hard behind ;
Nor yet the pleader's fluent tongue ;
Nor sweetest voice that ever sung ;
Nor noblest statesman's grasp of mind,
With will and energy combined ;
But virtues, less esteemed by most,
Though purchased at a higher cost :—
Fair PURITY takes foremost place—
Heart HOLINESS, not winsome face,—
No heart is brave till life is pure ;
All noble lives this truth make sure.
UNSELFISHNESS—a noble grace—
Must claim the right to second place ;
The heart of self must emptied be,
Before its power to help is free.
HUMILITY, sweet modest flower,
Must flourish in the heart's fair bower ;
All lofty pride, and love of pelf,
And all that magnifies one's self,
Must find no lurking-place within—
Must banished be, like mortal sin.
Sweet SYMPATHY, like soothing balm,
Must flow forth from a heart that's calm,

With gentleness and love o'erspread,
While PITY's tears are freely shed :
The great root grace must added be ;
These but the fruit, and FAITH the tree—
A constant ever-acting faith,
Which ever rests on, " Jesus saith."
The trusting heart has richest dower,
And aye can claim divinest power.
The heart that loves and trusts and prays,
And leans on God in all its ways,
Is never weak—must aye be strong—
Is ever filled with gladdening song.

A heart in fellowship with God
Will tread the path which Jesus trod ;
On LOVE His Kingdom He did found ;
'Twas LOVE that men's hearts to Him bound ;
The secret of His power we see
In sweet and loving sympathy.
He cared for men and sought their good ;
When hungry He provides them food ;
When sick their maladies He heals ;
To all by GENTLENESS appeals.
He comes to all as lowly, meek,
Nor place nor honour does He seek ;
When they would fain have made Him king,
No charm does such high offer bring.

But once He sat in Sanhedrim,
When learnèd Rabbis questioned Him;
A boy of twelve, He questions asked,
And learnèd Doctors' skill He tasked.
In this High Court He might have won
Such honour as was given to none;
But, lo! from it He turns away;
Nor place nor power can make Him stay;
He nothing sought that "great men" seek,
AND YET MEN CALLED NOT JESUS WEAK.

He seemed to choose a woman's place,
Nor ever cared to run a race
With men for honour and renown.
And why? He sought a higher crown.
He found His joy in doing good;
In feeding men with heavenly food;
In binding up the broken heart;
In giving erring a new start
In life, forgiving all the past,—
Their sins behind His back were cast.
A magic power did Jesus wield,—
Through LOVE His power was revealed.
Was Jesus WEAK, because He chose
To minister to human woes,
And turned away from place and power
To save the weak in trying hour?

Nay, 'mong the strong the strongest He,—
Such is the voice of History.
His Kingdom, solely built on LOVE,
To-day in might stands far above
All kingdom, formed in any way,
In ancient or in modern day.

Lo! Lily, this I've found at length :
What men call weakness is our strength ;
The greatest power, the rarest art,
Is power to win the human heart,—
To win it back from paths of sin,—
To make men clean and pure within ;
T' uplift the fallen, save the lost,
And comfort those by trouble tossed :
And WOMAN, strong in love and trust,
And, haply, free from worldly lust,
And full of PITY's gentleness,
Divinest power does possess
To stem the tide of wickedness,
And every human creature bless.
'Tis hers, with Jesus, forth to go
And save the world from sin and woe.

Leander, truly this is power,
If we could claim it as our dower.
But I have thought that one would need
One's self to be the Christ indeed

To do the things that Jesus did,
And live such noble life amid
The squalor and the misery
On every hand we daily see.
CAN WOMAN, cultured and refined,
Have love enough for human kind
To visit haunts of vice and sin,
And there seek human hearts to win ?

Yes, Lily, you do rightly weigh
This pressing problem, when you say
That one would need the Christ to be
To fraternize with misery ;
To take the fallen by the hand,
And pluck them, like a burning brand,
From Vice's slow, consuming fire ;
To labour on and never tire
Of stolid, thankless, graceless hearts,
Fast closed 'gainst our most winsome arts.

But may we not Christ's image wear ?
Yea, MUST we not, His name who bear ?
A CHRIST, each Christian in his sphere,
To men thus bringing Jesus near.
'Twas this that made the noble Paul,
Aye ready at the Master's call,
To suffer hardships, dangers brave,
In order precious souls to save.

" To me to live is Christ," he said ;
In Jesus' steps he sought to tread ;
Another Christ was he 'mong men,
Lo ! living out Christ's life again.
For, hark ! he says, " Christ lives in me ;
And I no longer live, but He :
He is my LIFE ; He moves my will ;
And with His Spirit doth me fill ;
His love is throbbing in my heart ;
Through HIS eyes I behold men's smart ;
His voice speaks tenderly through mine,
And clothes my words with power divine ;
His presence aye has nerved me on
To go where man could ne'er have gone."

Lo ! Lily, it does seem to me
That " other Christs " we all may be.
The noble Paul was but a man—
The bravest, true, since world began—
His strength he claimed not as his own ;
This truth he clearly has made known :
Each enterprise, in Christ begun,
In Him his victories were won.
In wondrous words we hear him claim
His triumphs in Immanuel's name :
" I can do all things through the Christ,
" Who strengthens me," by love enticed ;—

" Now thanks to God who always gives
" The victory to him who lives
" In constant fellowship with Christ,
" And daily keeps with Him his tryst."
Thus it would seem that Paul was made
Omnipotent by Jesus' aid ;
He's always victor in the fight,
Because endued with heavenly might.
And, lo ! the Christ—the Vine—has said,
" Apart from Me the branch is dead ;
" Abide in Me, and I in you ;
" Apart from Me ye naught can do :
" I am the Sap, the Stem, the Root,
" He who abides in Me bears fruit."
Paul laboured and all dangers dared,
Because the strength of Christ he shared ;
Hence this the burden of his song :
" When I am weak, then I am strong."
Strange paradox to intellect,—
'Tis strange to many, I suspect.

Lo ! Lily, this I've found to be
The law of Christian life for me :
Weak in myself, and prone to fall ;
But strong in Christ to conquer all.

Leander, is it here I find
The secret of your strength of mind,

Your power of will, your self-control,
Your happy heart and manly soul ?
Your life has always puzzled me—
Unselfish, brave, from worry free ;
Aye happy, generous, and kind—
Great strength and tenderness combined.
I reasoned thus : He is a man ;
And men are strong since time began.
Leander, was it always thus ?
Or were you ever weak, like us ?

Ah, Lily, I remember well,—
If my life's story I must tell,—
When strength and joy and self-control
Came flooding in upon my soul ;
From darkness deep as dead of night,
I entered into glorious light.
For weary months my soul was bowed
With grief's sad burden, though I vowed,
And wrestled hard, and wept, and prayed,
And pleaded with high Heaven for aid.
All wrong was banished from my life ;
With no one, but myself, at strife ;
A happy home, as youth could wish ;
Pure pleasures, sipped from many a dish ;
Friends—loving, thoughtful, generous, kind ;
But still, alas! no peace of mind.

The soul was crushed—no inward rest,
Though outwardly supremely blest.
'Twas passing strange the path I trod;
My one long quest was "PEACE WITH GOD."
I yearned and prayed, but no peace came;
I longed for Power, yet none could claim;
As helpless as an orphaned child,
I strayed in desert, lone and wild.
By stainless life I sought to gain
My heart's desire, but sought in vain;
My purity of life and heart
Increased, but never eased, my smart.
It daily crushed me more and more,
And pierced my heart to inmost core,
That life like mine, nor fault nor stain,
Should yield no fruit but ceaseless pain;
Yea, pain most painful of its kind,—
Not pain of body, but of mind,—
A ceaseless, longing, yearning cry;
O Saviour, hear, or I must die.

How slow the weary months dragged on!
My spark of life had almost gone!
No ray of hope, no foretaste given;
My anguished heart with grief still riven.

At length there came, like some sweet strain
Of angel-song, with glad refrain,

A voice to me, in bonds enslaved,
" Look unto Me, and be ye saved."
" LOOK UNTO ME! LOOK UNTO ME!"
" My life for thee! My life for thee!"
" Look not to SELF, nor aught of thine!
" But trust in LOVE and POWER divine,—
" A LOVE that freely pardons sin,—
" A POWER that makes all new within."
'Twas Jesus, speaking to my need,
And seeking my sad soul to lead
Out from its darkness and its gloom,
And from the awful dread of doom,
And let my ravished eyes behold
The GOODNESS and the LOVE untold
Of God as FATHER, HELPER, FRIEND,
Aye ready timely help to send.

Thus I was taught that sinners need
A Saviour,—One to intercede,—
A living, reigning Christ within
To subjugate and cast out sin.
By sore experience I had learned
That PEACE, for which I, longing, yearned,
Could not be found by strictest life,
So long as there was inward strife
Between the soul and God Most High:
To strive with God was but to die.

And, lo! there came to my sad soul,
As rippling sea-waves softly roll,
A revelation, glorious, sweet:
THY GOD IS LOVE, and it is meet
That HE supremely loved should be,
If you in peace His face would see.
Your friends you love, your books, and fame,—
Ambitious aye to win a name
In learning's walks,—in doing good,—
These more to you than daily food;
But God, your best and truest Friend,
Who did, in love, rich blessings send,
Endowing you, in heart and mind,
With gifts and graces rare combined,
YOU HAVE NOT LOVED, Whom not to love
Is sin all other sins above.
O wondrous word! O thrilling thought!
Lo! with profoundest meaning fraught!
True it shall stand while ages run:
NOT TO LOVE GOD ALL SINS IN ONE.

Ah, Lily, you astonished seem:
Say, do you think 'twas but a dream—
A muddled vision of the night,
Engendered by the soul's sad plight?

Leander, you misread my thought:
The story of your life has brought

In vivid light before my mind
A truth to which I've long been blind.
In your past life I see mine own ;
New light upon my path you've thrown.
Like you, it aye has been my aim
In SELF all power for good to claim.
By energy and earnestness
I hoped the world to help and bless ;
But all my efforts fruitless fell,—
My failures—more than tongue can tell.
The cause of failure I did seek,—
And then pronounced all women weak.
Alas! I fear, though aim was high,
My motive reached not to the sky.
The path of truth and right I trod ;
But did not serve from love to God.
Your words touch tender chords within :
" NOT TO LOVE GOD IS DEEPEST SIN."
Leander, do you mean to say
That thought like this has been your stay—
Has given you such strength and power—
Has all these years been your strong tower ?

Lo! Lily, this transcendent truth
I've held most dear since early youth ;
With it my life of strength began :
" NOT TO LOVE GOD ALL SINS IN ONE."

C

'Twas first sure step to glorious light
From chilling gloom and starless night.
It oped my eyes and let me see,
That stainless life might sinful be;
The life nor fault nor flaw might show,
And yet no POWER forth from it flow;
From active service never cease,
And yet, within, no well of peace.

But, Lily, would you fully know
The secret source whence POWER doth flow:
Another step, in glorious guise,
Was taken ere I seized the prize.
The instant that momentous word
The fountain of my heart had stirred,
I saw that GOODNESS I had none,—
" NOT TO LOVE GOD ALL SINS IN ONE."
Unworthy, loveless, Oh, how vile!—
Responding not to God's sweet smile!
Not loving Him, Who so loved me!
Who proved His love on Calvary's tree!
Oh! heart of hardness! heart of stone!
Oh! how could heart so hard have grown!
And, lo! my loveless heart was still
Most gentle, tender, would ev'n thrill
And fill at sight of human woe,—
More blind it was than hard, I trow.

To love a God far-off, unseen,
Unknown to FAITH and HOPE, I ween,
Is hardest of all hard things given
To man to do beneath high Heav'n.
I could not love—could only cry :
" O Jesus ! save me ere I die !
" All helpless at Thy feet I fall !
" In mercy hear me, as I call !
" I own that nothing good I've done :—
" Not to love God all sins in one !
" A sinner ! save by Thy great grace !
" Forgive !   Forgive !   And Thy sweet face
" In love reveal, that I may love
" And serve like saints in Heaven above ! "

In answer to my yearning cry
I felt a glorious PRESENCE nigh :
No tongue can tell, nor words convey
Ev'n glimpse of glory seen that day.
The PRESENCE my whole heart did fill,
And whispered softly, " PEACE, BE STILL."
And O such peace ! such calm within !
Most certain pledge of pardoned sin !
Most glorious freedom !   Heavenly light !
A glory making all things bright,
And beautiful, and fair to see !
'Twas Heaven itself come down to me !

And, lo ! this glorious inner light
Transfigured Nature to my sight :
For, seeing God as reconciled,
And, being owned as His own child,
My ravished eyes new vision found,
And BEAUTY held me all around.
My heart with fondest love was filled ;
And LOVE TO GOD did Nature gild
With glorious beauty, Heaven's dower,—
Each blade had charm, like rarest flower,—
All-glorious—things great and small,—
My loving Father made them all.

And with this inner calm and peace,
And joy that never knew surcease,
And constant fellowship with Christ,
And sweetest faith, and love unpriced,
There also rolled, as sea-waves roll,
A wondrous peace in on my soul.
And, lo ! 'twas mighty to subdue
The WILL and PASSION,—to renew
The HEART, and change DESIRE—
Baptizing all with HOLY FIRE.
Such day can come but once to man ;
Nor does it need to come again :
It clean subdues all inward strife,
And makes the weakest strong for life.

PART II

TRIAL AND CONSECRATION.

LEANDER, lo! since last we met
I've pondered much, and ponder yet,
The things o'er which we talked and prayed,
Imploring Heaven's gracious aid.
Your story thrilled me through and through,
Revealing much to me that's new.
Day after day it filled my mind;
My yearning heart for POWER pined;
Those searching words held me within:
"Not to love God is deepest sin."
Perplexed, sore puzzled, deep distressed,
Why I, who was supremely blest
With gentle heart and love to man,
Should be so long placed under ban,—
Should be so powerless for good,
That I despised my womanhood,—
In deepest anguish Christ I sought,
And asked Him that I might be taught
The way to perfect PEACE and POWER;
For this I knew was Heaven's dower.

All confidence in self was gone,—
"Not to love God all sins in one;"—
I keenly felt with anguished heart,
That my whole life was wrong from start;
To self I looked for strength and power,
Instead of Christ as my strong tower.

Through weary days my soul was crushed;
At length there came sweet voice that hushed
My questionings and anxious fears,
While my whole soul was bathed in tears.
I prayed your prayer, and cried your cry:
" O Jesus, help me, or I die!"
" And quick the answer came with power:
" The Name of God is your strong tower—
" A tower of help in time of need,
" For Jesus is a Friend indeed,—
" A Friend that sticketh close as brother;
" Those who have Him will need no other."

The still small voice was soft and sweet,
And there was sound of angel-feet;
A hushed, strange PRESENCE filled the room,
And my sad soul did quick illume.
And now there came a glorious light
To mind and heart, where erst was night;
The sun in glory it outshone;
It bade all doubt and fear begone.

'Twas heavenly glory all around,—
A stillness, yet a low, soft sound,—
Sweet music, like of angel-choir ;
Within a strange, refining fire.

Lo ! Lily, it was Jesus Christ,
Who kept with you His promised tryst :
"Come unto Me, ye souls oppressed,
"Ye weary, I will give you rest."
'Twas such a PRESENCE Moses felt,
When he in PRAYER for Israel knelt :
"Thy PRESENCE must be our defence,
"Else, Lord, us carry not up hence."
His prayer was heard, the answer came—
A Voice from the Shekinah-flame—
"My PRESENCE aye shall be thy Guest,
"And truly I shall give thee rest."

Leander, can such glory last,—
Such heavenly peace, and power so vast,—
Such glorious fulness, perfect love,
Abounding life, like saints' above ?
Can our frail hearts for long contain
Such fulness and endure the strain ?
When came the answer to my cry,
The glory was so great, that I
Had almost prayed, like one of yore :
"Hold, Lord, for I can hold no more."

One almost trembles at the thought,
That work like this in one is wrought;
It seems ev'n more than great New Birth;
Yea, ev'n like Heav'n brought down to Earth.
Can one, so full of joy and bliss,
Remain, and toil in world like this?

Yes, Lily, 'tis most glorious state,
Which makes our hearts aye gravitate
To heavenly loves and pure desire,—
For Christ within is cleansing fire;—
But think not that your course is run,
For life to you is but begun.
This glorious life of PEACE and POWER
Is normal, for 'tis Heaven's dower.

Like Peter, on fair Hermon's height,
Enraptured by the glorious sight
Of visitors in heavenly sheen,
And Christ transfigurèd between,
You feel that glory such as this
Can only be preserved in bliss.
Like him, you say, for your own sake,
"Let us three tabernacles make;
"No more let us go down 'mong men
"To toil and struggle there again;
"Here I would rest, whate'er betide,
"And 'mid these glorious scenes abide."

Lo! Peter's selfish musings showed
Unfitness for such blest abode;
Experiences such as these
Are not bestowed ourselves to please.
Such power is given to be used
In blessing others; 'tis abused
If spent in storing joy and bliss;
In acting thus we're most remiss.
To Peter Jesus quick denied
The selfish bliss for which he sighed;
The glory vanished from his sight;
The heavenly visitors took flight;
The Master turned to earth again;
Once more He sought the haunts of men.

Such lofty moods to men are given,
Not to prepare the soul for Heaven
But to equip for nobler work;
And all remains of self that lurk
Within to banish from the life,
And cleanse the soul from inward strife.
This glorious peace, this joy and power,
Are but the opening buds; the flower
Aye comes with service; then much fruit,
Where FAITH and LOVE have ta'en deep root.

Lo! Lily, JOY and PEACE abide,
If we, like Jesus, turn aside

From pleasure's path and selfish ease,—
Each day refusing self to please—
And consecrate our life, our all,
Aye ready at the Master's call
To serve our fellows, save the lost,
Aye toiling, counting not the cost;
A blessed fulness He bestows
On those who care for other's woes.
Thus only we in Him abide;
For FAITH and LOVE, like flowimg tide,
Flow on and out to other hearts :
We cease to serve, our POWER departs.
God will not have His grace abused ;
He gives not POWER, except 'tis used ;
" No Waste " is first of Heaven's rules,—
To squander is the work of fools.
If, therefore, we would POWER retain,—
Have PEACE and JOY within us reign—
We must go forth, as Jesus went—
Aye spending, willing to be spent,
That precious souls, by sin enslaved,
May be sought out, and blessed, and saved.

'Tis fruit the gardener seeks; the flower
Is sweet to sense ; but where there's power
And life abundant, fruit is sought—
" Much fruit," said Jesus ;" thus is brought

"To God much praise; so ye shall be
" My own disciples—one with Me ;
" Yea, one with Me in LOVE and POWER,
" And one with Me in fruit and flower."
Yes, beautiful our lives must be
In meekness and humility,
In love and sweet simplicity,
In holiness and purity.
These all are flowers of sweetest bloom,
Emitting rich and rare perfume.
But fruitful, too, each life will be,
If grafted branch in the true Tree.
Hence Jesus said, " Abide in Me—
" Yes, thou in Me, and I in thee—
" For ye can yield nor flower nor fruit,
" If Sap flow not from Stem and Root."

In every heart where Christ doth dwell,
Sweet peace will flow, as from deep well :
But, that our Lord may dwell within,
We precious souls must seek to win.
While Jesus trod this sin-cursed earth
His life was active, ev'n from birth ;
And, when He dwells in human hearts,
This active goodness He imparts ;
So, Lily, your sweet joy and peace,
If they would never know surcease

Must be linked on to loving deeds,—
To sympathy with human needs ;
To tender care for souls oppressed :
To zeal in making others blessed ;
To self-denial for the poor ;—
Thus only can true joy endure.
To be LIKE CHRIST your aim must be,
If you would have Him dwell in thee.

Leander, now all this is plain,
Though once such words to me seemed vain ;
The glory that has filled my heart
None but the Christ could e'er impart.
Like Paul, with Him I keep my tryst,
And daily sing, " TO LIVE IS CHRIST."
His LOVE surpasses heart's desire ;
His PRESENCE is refining fire.
And now the joy of doing good
Is more to me than needful food ;
His PRESENCE daily strength supplies,
And SOULS makes precious in my eyes ;
Mankind seems brother to my heart,
I long to ease his pain and smart,—
To lead sad souls to Jesus' feet,
For I and they in Jesus meet.
And, lo ! my words are clothed with power ;
And oft, like sweet refreshing shower,

Bring joy and comfort to lone hearts :
My presence, ev'n, fresh strength imparts.

But I have felt at times distressed,
That failure had to be confessed ;
My bounding heart with love o'erflows,
I long to reach their deepest woes :
I tell them of a Saviour's love,
And point them to the rest above ;
I tell them of my changèd life,
Now free from care and inward strife :
How Jesus filled my heart with peace,
And from all sin gave sweet release—
Assuring them that He will do
The same for all, and them renew,
If they but truly seek His face,
And, yielding all, trust in his grace ;
And then there comes such tale of woe,
As makes one's heart in tears outflow.

A bright young life, once filled with song,
Quick blighted by most cruel wrong,—
Perfidious loves and treacherous wiles,
And artful schemes all wreathed in smiles ;
Deceived, deluded, led astray ;
Then left forlorn in dire dismay ;—
A timid, shrinking, blighted thing—
Neught left of life except its sting.

I yearn to comfort such sad heart,
But all experience and art
Alike are helpless to impart
A ray of hope, or heal its smart.
A knowing look and pitying tone
Reveal how much one life has known
Of deepest anguish, crushing woe:
" Ah, miss, you're kind, but nothing know
" Of sorrow, suffering, loss, despair;
" Of broken heart, unanswered prayer;
" Of Poverty's heart-piercing stare ;
" Of crushing toil, and ceaseless care.
" You have not suffered ; have you, Miss ?
" You have not been in plight like this ?"

My lips were sealed ; I shook my head,
Assenting to the words she said.
All helpless, speechless, there I stood—
Alas ! so weak is womanhood !
Why could I not find words to bless
A sister in such dire distress ?
I longed to comfort, yearned to save ;
Yet naught but useless tears I gave.

Ah, Lily, there's one lesson more—
A precious lesson kept in store—
Which you, perchance, may have to learn ;
For which you will not cease to yearn,

When its high value once you know,—
'Tis priceless dower, though born of woe.
YOURSELF MUST SUFFER; you must feel
In your own heart the piercing steel.
Know, if CONSOLER you would be,
That hearts yield quick to sympathy.
Not yearning heart and Christly ways,
Nor yet Affection's earnest gaze;
Not tearful Pity's tenderness,
Nor Love alone the sad can bless;
But SYMPATHY, like soothing balm,
Must flow forth from a heart that's calm
And confident, because it knows
The deepest depths of human woes:
Because itself has suffered loss,
Has borne with meekness many a cross;
And from the depths has risen again,
Enriched, ennobled by the pain
And agony and loss endured,
And now can speak in words assured.
Such heart alone can sympathize,—
Can feeling show in tone and eyes,—
Can know how best to give relief;
Because it knows the depths of grief.

The sister, whom you sought to bless,
Had fathomed depths of deep distress;

She quick discerned where you were weak,—
Not weak in love—in words to speak;
But weak, though blessed with rarest art,
To touch within her bruisèd heart,
A single sympathetic chord
By Pity's tear, or Love's kind word.
A world of meaning, all should know,
Lies hidden 'neath those words of woe:
"You have not suffered; have you, Miss?
"You have not been in plight like this?"

Leander, must I suffer then;
Must I withdraw my hand again
From service, till I suffer loss,
And pain, and bear the cross?
My greatest loss and keenest pain—
More galling than foul slavery's chain—
Would surely be to be denied
The joy, more than all joy beside,
Of helping heavy-laden hearts,
And shielding them from Tempter's darts;
Of leading them to Jesus' feet,
And making them for Heaven meet.
And yet 'tis true what you have said;
My weakness I shall ever dread,
Until each heart, with sorrow wrung,
Shall find in me both heart and tongue

Responsive to its direst woes,
While active sympathy outflows,—
Till I shall probe the depths of pain,
And more than former strength regain.

Leander, I have wondered oft
How you are proudly borne aloft
In trying scenes, and ready aye
From sad hearts grief to roll away.
Has suffering been your rich dower?
Is this the secret of your power?
Have you passed through all human woes,
And felt mankind's heart-throbs and throes?
Have you met trial, suffered loss—
Betimes borne down by crushing cross?

Yes, Lily, 'tis as you have said;
With sorrow's bread I have been fed:
What fulness I may have possessed,
And skill in making others blessed,
And sympathy with troubled hearts,
And power to shield from Tempter's darts,
I trace to being wisely led
Along a pathway thickly spread
With trouble, trial, sorrow, pain,
Which sorely tried both heart and brain.

D

In College days my sore began;
For weary months it ceaseless ran;
For peering Doubt tried hard to roll
Its dread dead weight in on my soul.

'Twas like another self within,
And scarcely seemed allied to sin.
Betimes I thought it "thing of evil"—
Direct temptation of the devil;
Again I found my questionings good,
For mind and brain the richest food.
They made me summon all my skill
To check and crush thoughts seeming ill;
And Wisdom's treasures oft unlock
To keep my feet firm on the ROCK.
They made me dig, as for fine gold,
For hidden treasures, new and old,
In doctrines, precepts, promises,
Revealed and given by God to bless
Sad seeking souls, by doubt oppressed,
That they might be supremely blest.

All golden truths by God revealed,
That oft did precious comfort yield,
In testing crucible were cast,
To see if they the fiery blast
Of Reason, Science, could withstand,
And Criticism's high demand.

Could God be LOVE and punish sin—
Hereditary taint within ;
Is there from such law no escape ?
Shall fathers eat the sour grape,
And children's teeth be set on edge ?
That this is justice who would pledge ?
Such problem stared me in the face—
Most strange it seemed, apart from grace—
But deeper thought helped me to see
Rich blessing in heredity.
For parents there was motive strong,
To live pure lives and hand along
A blessing to posterity,
By sure law of heredity.
The law that works for good *is* good,
Although, perverted, it gives food
And fuel to all natures base,
And gives to evil larger place.
The law is good that can make sure
That parents, whose own lives are pure,
Will give to children nobler dower
To save them from temptation's power.
And God, in love to fallen man,
Wrought out His great redemption plan,
Whereby the past is all forgiven ;
Whereby Sin's fetters quick are riven ;
Whereby through union to the Christ,
New life and power and love unpriced

To man are given; in Christ he stands—
Secure from all the Law's demands—
More strong and safe than Adam stood,
Or Eve in her pure womanhood.

Leander, 'tis a blessing, then,
For doubt to wrestle with strong men.
It gave you nobler views of God,—
A loving purpose, not a rod
Of chastening, in grief you found,
Which you to God more strongly bound.

But, lo! had we to wrestle thus,
What havoc it would make with us!
We women do not argue things;
For LOVE, with FAITH, around us flings
A screen to break the tempest's force:
Unquestioning faith our last resource.

Yes, Lily, as a thing of course,
Your LOVE and FAITH your last resource.
And 'tis your first and only plea;
And such as you we men should be.
In all my questionings and doubt
Strong Reason put no foe to rout;
'Twas LOVE and FAITH of early days—
Which filled my heart with joy and praise

And memories left, as sweet as song—
That, in my trial, made me strong.
This one great fact stood out most bright,
And oft turned darkness into light :
The loving Christ had heard my cries,
And all my groanings and my sighs
Had changed to songs.   My heart He filled
With gladness ; all unrest He stilled ;
My PEACE a Heaven of delight ;
The tide of JOY stood at full height.
Then Christ most real was to me,
More near than human friend could be.
LOVE knew no bounds—to Him be thanks—
Like Jordan, it o'erflowed its banks ;
And FAITH rose up like stately tower,
And strongest was in darkest hour ;
And, ev'n when came severest shock,
HOPE's anchor held to Christ, the Rock.
Not REASON was the cable strong,
That held my barque, when borne along
'Mong breakers DOUBT's fierce tempest raised ;
But LOVE and FAITH, with hands upraised
To Him who hears the silent sigh,
The whispered prayer, the yearning cry.
Yes, Lily, FAITH *my* last resource
To break the tempest's crushing force.
Had Jesus not been real to me ;
Had FAITH's eye not been quick to see

In Him an ever-present Friend,
Aye near in trial to defend,—
The torch of REASON in such night
Could give the soul no ray of light.
In Christ alone can we be strong;
In sorrow He alone gives song;
In darkness He to us is light
'Tis He Who gives "songs in the night."

Leander, were your trials such
As only INTELLECT to touch?
Or, has your HEART been wrung with pain
At loss of friends to glory ta'en?
You show such tenderness in grief,
And are so quick to give relief
To sad lone hearts, that I have thought
Such sympathy had been inwrought
In you by some most trying loss,
As hard to bear as death on cross.
You seem to know all human woes;
Your heart in sympathy outgoes
To every form of human grief,
As if men's woes were but a leaf
Of your life-story, written plain
In ink of blood upon your brain.
You must have suffered grief at heart,
And conquered all its pains and smart.

Trial and Consecration.

You must have felt, in every form,
The startling shock of Grief's rough storm.

True, Lily, I have felt Pain's dart
In Body, Intellect, and Heart;
And in this order came the pain.
On bed of sickness I had lain
In early youth, till all seemed o'er;
I almost stood upon the shore
Of Sea Eternal.   As was meet
It laid me low at Jesus' feet.
My vows were heard; my life was spared;
To live a holy life I dared.
And now, with health restored at length,
My weakness proved true source of strength;
I saw my life was not my own,—
A gift from God, 'twas His alone,
To be recalled at any hour
By Him Whose wisdom matched His power.

'Twas good to rise 'bove stinging pain;
'Twas good new Life and Power to gain;
But better far to yield up all,—
My life, my service, at His call,—
To give to Him the sole control
Of Heart, and Intellect, and Soul;
To be and do whate'er He willed;
To have in me each day fulfilled

Whate'er He purposèd and planned;
To realise that His eye scanned
My daily path and led me on
In footprints where my Lord had gone.

My CONSECRATION was entire:
Hence I was filled with heavenly fire;
The heart was cleansed; with peace was filled;
And every anxious fear was stilled:
To live for Christ I now desired—
To perfect HOLINESS aspired;
And O how glorious was the REST!
My erst sad soul supremely blest!
This but FIRST step—the flesh subdued,—
The heart with heavenly LOVE imbued.

In CONSECRATION ALL is laid
Upon the altar; and 'tis said:
The altar sanctifies the gift;—
'Tis sacred, and no hand dare lift
From off the altar what is given,
Without displeasure from high Heaven.
When loving heart yields all to Christ,
It must be faithful to its tryst:
It may not know how much was laid
Upon the altar LOVE had made;
But ALL is Christ's by LOVE's free gift,
With CONSECRATION's hands uplift;

There all must lie and bide His will,
His mandate ready to fulfil.
The flesh was tried, and yielded all—
" Or life or death " at Jesus' call.

A few short seasons quick have passed ;
The mind has been expanding fast :
AMBITION seeks to win a name ;
Proud INTELLECT asserts its claim ;
It roams the world in quest of food ;
It soars to Heaven for highest good :
Divine Philosophy it scans,
And seeks to know God's secret plans ;—
Would question the All-Wise, and try
To argue—know the reason why
Man was so made, with downward trend ;
And how could God be his true Friend ?

Such daring must needs meet rebuff ;
For had not He revealed enough
Of His great love to me in Christ,—
Who ever kept with me His tryst,—
Who had so filled my longing soul,
And cleansed and fortified the whole ?
Was not the Mighty God revealed
In Him as LOVE ?   Had he not sealed
My yearning heart by the great dower
Of His own Spirit, giving POWER ?

To me He showed Himself as LOVE;
As Cleansing Spirit, Heavenly Dove;
As POWER and MIGHT to conquer ill;
And thus with PEACE my heart did fill.
And why should INTELLECT demand
A clearer vision at His hand?
This Revelation is the best
With which man can on earth be blest.

God was revealed in written Word;
But this, true PEACE did not afford.
Then Jesus came as man 'mong men,
And thus revealed true God again:
" He that sees Me the Father sees;
" For I do always seek to please
" The Father; and I thus reveal,
" To all to whom My words appeal,
" His love, His sympathy, His heart,
" And thus true views of God impart."

Yet nearer still God draws to men;
For Jesus, ta'en to Heaven again,
Returns, as Spirit, with new POWER
In man to dwell, as noblest dower
Of life, and strength, and HOLINESS,—
Best gift with which God man can bless.
This Revelation, choicest, best,
With which mere mortal e'er is blest,

To me was given; His mighty power
My life renewed in one short hour.
In sweet experience I had known
That God had made my heart His throne;
Yet INTELLECT with madding pride,
From simple FAITH would turn aside
To reason, argue, mysteries try
To solve with closed or half-oped eye;
For INTELLECT is blind to see
The great and precious mystery
Of man in Christ to God allied,
Or how in man Christ can abide.
These precious truths to men are known
By heart-experience alone.
As thing of course proud INTELLECT
Was baffled, fretted, well-nigh wrecked
On Doubt's strange rocks and reefs and shoals,
While dark Despair's sea o'er it rolls.
So INTELLECT must yield its claim,
And meekly bow 'fore Jesus' name—
Must let the Christ be all in all,
And humbly trust, whate'er befall.
This SECOND step, when INTELLECT
With FAITH's bright flowers herself has decked.

   Nor yet was victory complete:
The HEART must lie at Jesus' feet,—
Whate'er He asks must gladly yield
Before it fullest POWER can wield.

Yea, all that's to AFFECTION dear,—
Ev'n love the purest, most sincere—
In CONSECRATION must be laid
Upon the altar.   I had prayed
That His sweet will might ever be,
By Joy or Grief, fulfilled in me.
This is true CONSECRATION'S prayer;
And yet we may be scarce aware
How large the sweep of such request
Until by trial sorely pressed.
God wills that we should meekly bow
Our wills to His, whene'er we vow,
In all things that concern our peace,
That anxious care may ever cease.

When we have freely yielded all—
Self—service—to the Master's call;
We each must tested be and tried
To prove that we to self have died.
The trial, though 'tis hard to bear,
Is God's response to our own prayer.
'Tis well that it should be severe,
And thus forever banish fear.
When to the HEART sore trial comes,
And all its deepest depths it plumbs,
'Tis, by that act, made strong for life,
And never more knows aught of strife.
If trustful HEART its dearest treasure
Yields up, unmurmuring, at God's pleasure,

That act sublime all self subdues ;
And now the HEART and WILL will choose
The will of God, so far as known ;
His right to rule will gladly own.

Leander, can one bear such smart—
This testing trial of the HEART ?
Can woman, sensitive and weak,
Dare pray your prayer, and your words speak :
"That God's sweet will might ever be,
" By Joy or Grief, fulfilled in thee ? "
We're crushed when with dear friends we part :
Can dearest treasure of the heart
Be yielded up, without complaint,
By modern Stoic, or by saint ?
Can woman shield her throbbing heart,
And make it proof 'gainst Sorrow's dart ?
Could I prove true the words you speak,
No more would I call woman " weak."
Leander, do you know the cost
At which one's dearest treasure's lost ?

Ah, Lily, if to *feel* the blow ;
Or, if to *suffer* is to know ;
Then, verily, I know the cost
At which the dearest treasure 's lost.
One dearer than all else beside,—
Whose modest worth no art could hide,

Whose gentleness was known to all,
In holy zeal another Paul,
As winsome as sweet face could be,
Aye robed in spotless purity,—
A flower of fairest promise, given
To bud on Earth, to bloom in Heaven,—
Was plucked from out Earth's garden fair
To bloom for aye in purer air.
Most unexpected was the blow;
'Twas sudden, startling, crushing woe.
Why was she taken—she who gave
Abundant promise souls to save?
True, she was ripe for life in Heaven;
And yet Earth needed such sweet leaven.
Such 'JOY IN JESUS,' seldom seen,
Was like the glorious golden sheen
Of setting sun on summer eve,—
Such web of life as angels weave,—
Not like the fainter glow of morn,
Which one is wont to see adorn
The life of those still young in years—
Though bright betimes, oft dimmed with tears.

Leander, why did God not spare
Such life in answer to your prayer?

Lo! Lily, God is good, although
His secrets mortals may not know.

'Twas strange indeed how on such day
To spare such life I did not pray.
My prayer—each day I made request—
Was that my darling might be blessed;
That God's sweet will might aye be done
In her and me till crown was won.
His will was that a noble life,
Full of good deeds and free from strife,
By early death might speak to men
With more persuasive voice than when
That pleading voice, by word and song,
Was soothing, cheering, making strong
Lone sufferers in attic bare;
In crowded close with putrid air;
In hospital, and private room,
Which radiant face did oft illume.
And, when her Lord would call her home,
The tossing waves, with crests of foam,
Between us rolled; I did not know,
Ev'n by presentiment of woe,
That life beyond physician's skill
Had quickly passed; but, by God's will,
Had fondly hoped in three short days
To bask again in the bright rays
Of radiant face with Heaven-lit smile:
Alas! alas! that "little while!"

By purpose high I did not know
Fell fever's fire had laid her low ;
I then believed ; I still believe
That PRAYER its wonders can achieve ;
The Prayer of Faith I could have prayed
Her case before the Lord have laid
In fullest confidence that He
Such precious life would spare to me.
Once Moses, holy man and great—
To save his people from sad fate—
Raised holy hands to God and prayed
That His fierce anger might be stayed,
Till answer came, " Let Me alone,
That my hot wrath may quick be known."
So, had I then been by her side ;
Could I have seen life's ebbing tide ;
To God in faith I could have prayed—
And Him have highest honour paid—
Until " Let Me alone " was said,
And life was claimed from realms of dead.
But that His purpose, good and wise,
Unhindered by my faith and cries,
Might be fulfilled, He so ordained,
In sweetest ruth and love unfeigned,
That she should reach her home on high,
Ere I should know such change was nigh.

Such was the trial of my HEART:
As keen and piercing as Grief's dart
Has ever been in heart of man,—
A strange, perplexing, puzzling plan
Of God, all-knowing and all-wise,
Wrought out in unexpected guise.
That fateful day no more could do,
If all the Fates should hard pursue;
The loss of all things dear to me
Would have been naught, if only she,
More dear to me than all beside,
Were left—a treasure to abide.

Leander, 'twas too much to bear:
The mere recital makes me share
Your bitter loss.   Lo! Pity's tear
Fast trickles down my cheek! Oh, dear!
But how did you endure the strain?
Or, how your wonted faith regain?
Did you not murmur and repine?
Or, could you bow to Will Divine?

Yes, Lily, bowed to Will Divine:
"My Father, not my will, but Thine!"
No fretting, chafing, 'neath the blow:
"My loving Father wills it so!"
"He loves me, and His Will is best;
"Who trusts Him is supremely blest."

E

Yet, truly, it was hard to bear—
A blank in life beyond repair;
But, still, in loneliest, saddest hour,
My heart would feel a sweet, strange POWER—
A wondrous PRESENCE, giving peace,
And causing anxious care to cease.
'Twas Jesus, coming in His grace
To make my heart His dwelling-place:
Now emptied of its richest treasure,
His fulness fills it beyond measure.

And now the victory is complete;
The heart aye lies at Jesus' feet;
Whate'er He asks, it gladly yields,
And gracious POWER ever wields:
It chimes its own sweet melody;
'Tis full of LOVE and SYMPATHY:
It feels for human misery;
And crushed hearts sets at liberty.
No fretting care does e'er intrude;
'Tis full of joy in doing good;
The living Christ aye dwells within,
And keeps the heart from conscious sin:
HEART, FLESH, and INTELLECT subdued,
" All things together work for good."

Leander, must we all be tried,
Ere perfect PEACE will aye abide

Within our oft-distracted hearts,—
Ere God His gracious power imparts
To keep the soul in trying hour,
Enriching it with Heaven's best dower?
And must we suffer loss and pain,
That we deep sympathy may gain?
Is there no other path to POWER—
No other way to our "strong tower?"
Must FLESH, and INTELLECT, and HEART,
Each feel the thrust of Trial's dart?
Must all the Consecrated tread
The path along which you were led?

Lo! Jesus lived the pattern life—
No carking care—no inward strife;
The path along which He was led
The Consecrated all must tread.
He Trial and Temptation met—
Was by the devil sore beset;
His trial was a triple dart
To test FLESH, INTELLECT, and HEART:
"You're hungry make of stone some bread,
"That 'Son of God' be fitly fed":

"Man does not live by bread alone;
"Why, then, should I make bread from stone?
"The Father's Will to Me is food:
"To please Him is the highest good."

Presumptuous daring next was tried
By Tempter, but was thrust aside;
The INTELLECT rejects his nod:
" Thou shalt not tempt the Lord thy God."

The HEART the Tempter next assails
With bribe of proffered power, but fails :
" Give me Thy Love, and worship me :
" Lo ! Kingdoms I will give to Thee " !

" Such Honour is for God alone ;
" His sway all Hearts must gladly own."

Three times Satanic skill He foiled :
Three times proud Satan's words recoiled
Upon himself.   Christ victory gained ;
His three-fold nature still unstained.
His Sword, the Word of God, He whet ;
The Tempter with a Text He met.
" In all points tempted like as we,"
He bore the palm of victory.
Lo ! then " the devil leaveth Him,"
While on Him wait the Cherubim.

The Christ-Experience must be ours,
If we would summon all our powers
For highest service 'mongst mankind,
And broken, bleeding hearts upbind.

Temptation's scalpel must dissect
The FLESH, and HEART, and INTELLECT:
By God's help each must victory claim;
And triumph in Immanuel's Name.
Lo! all the powers of HEART, and SOUL,
And WILL and INTELLECT—the whole
Must be, with LOVE'S fair flowers arrayed,
On CONSECRATION'S altar laid:
Then PEACE and POWER shall reign within:
The Living Christ shall vanquish sin;
The "wicked one" us shall not touch:
For on, nor broken reed nor crutch
We lean for strength, but on THE CHRIST,
Whose LOVE hath us imparadised.

PART III.

THE LIFE OF FAITH.

LEANDER, long I've sought such dower—
This REST of FAITH and conscious POWER;
And since this POWER is not our own,
It need not dwell in man alone.
Your teaching now to me seems plain,
It honours Christ, and breaks my chain.
The LIVING CHRIST may dwell within
A Woman's heart. Thus she may win
Divine and Christly skill and power
To bless sad hearts in darkest hour.
My weakness in the past has been
That on the Christ I did not lean.
I trusted to my love and zeal,
My skilful tact and strong appeal,
To win men from their evil ways:
By kindly deeds I won their praise.
Alas! although they thought me kind,
My counsels they seemed not to mind.
My life, my love, my kindly speech
Lacked power their consciences to reach.

The POWER I want, in Christ you've found:
Here I would seek sure standing ground.

   Yes, Lily, Christ must be your POWER:
You must receive His Spirit's dower
In all His fulness.   He your heart
Must touch, and Holy Fire impart.
His constant presence you must seek;
His words your lips must ever speak.
He who gave PARDON, PERFECT PEACE,
And JOY in WORK, will yet increase
Your dower of gifts, if you but live
The Life of Faith; for God doth give
To trustful, consecrated hearts
A glorious fulness.   He imparts
The life abundant, and doth thrill
The heart by touch Divine,—doth fill
To overflowing every soul
That gives to Him the sole control
Of HEART and WILL;—when every thought
To His sweet will is captive brought.

   Leander, can we live such life
On this side Heav'n, where sin is rife?
O how I've prayed and yearned to see
Such glorious work wrought out in me!
Sweet foretaste has to me been given;
I seemed transported into Heaven:

I wondered if such joy could last;
I thought to see it ebbing fast,
Like ebbing tide receding far,—
Mere glimpse of Heav'n through gates ajar.

Lo! Lily, JOY and POWER may last,
If all our cares on Christ we cast;
If daily we in Him abide,
And from his LOVE ne'er turn aside;
If we in all things Him obey,
And closely follow Him each day.
Like you, I wondered if this PEACE,
So glorious, should never cease.
In sweet experience, lo! I found
A heavenly glory all around—
An inner JOY before unknown,—
Such JOY as they around the Throne
On High might know; such sweet control—
A glorious Sabbath for the soul.
And, lo! this LIFE of LOVE did last;
For fleeting months and years have passed,
And ne'er has murmur passed my lips;
And ne'er has FAITH known an eclipse.
Each trial finds me calm and strong;
The darkest night has sweetest song.
Brave Paul's brave words are ever true:
" By grace of God I aye can do

"All things through Christ Who strengthens me :"
The Father's Hand in all I see.

Those who enjoy the REST of FAITH
Have all one watchword: " JESUS SAITH :"
They trust His promise, " Come to Me,
And I sweet REST will give to thee ;"
They trust His LEADING and His LIGHT,
For they have learned that he leads right ;
They trust His POWER, for they know
He's strong to conquer every foe ;
They trust His WISDOM, for each day
His glorious LIGHT illumes the way ;
They trust His KEEPING and His CARE,
And they are kept from every snare ;
His PRESENCE gives them POWER within,
And they are kept from conscious sin :
They know that they are one with Christ,
And life becomes imparadised.

Leander, this is noble dower—
This REST of FAITH, this conscious POWER.
In service does it ever fail ?
Do doubts and fears the heart assail ?
When you have pleaded and have prayed
That, by the Holy Spirit's aid,
Your spoken words may reach the heart,
And by God's grace, new life impart ;

And then behold no change in life—
No freedom from Sin's power and strife—
In those to whom your message came,
Whom you are yearning to reclaim
From Sin's dark, dreary, downward way,
And bring back to Eternal Day;
Does not Faith's wings begin to tire,
And oft refuse to bear you higher?
And does not FAILURE quench the fire
Of zeal, and oft detune HOPE's lyre;
So that its highest, brighest notes
Cannot be struck?   The music floats
Too low to bear aloft the soul
To fleckless skies—serenest goal?
'Tis FAILURE that sore puzzles me,
Since POWER DIVINE is full and free.

But, Lily, what does " FAILURE " mean ?
If I on God do daily lean
For strength and guidance, and am led
In pathway which my Lord did tread,
And do each day what pleases Him,
Why should the eye of Faith grow dim?
Why should Hope's anchor lose its hold?
Why should my love and zeal grow cold?
And why should fell Despair's cold chill
Creep o'er my soul—my bosom fill

The Life of Faith.

With anxious care and doubt and fear,
And from Love's eye draw trickling tear,
Although no fruit may yet appear
My longing, trusting heart to cheer ?
Our loving service ne'er can be
A "failure," if, obedient, we
Our Father please, and do His will.
If we, in faith, let Him fulfil
In us His purpose, good and wise,
Our lives are pleasing in His eyes.
Lo ! We may trust His faithfulness :
And whether "failure," or "success,"
In haste upon our work we write,
If it be pleasing in His sight,
We need not worry or repine,
But trust to LOVE and POWER Divine
To cause the seed we sow to root,
And, in His time, bring forth the fruit.

Leander, these are goodly words :
Like sweetest notes of singing birds
They sweeten life and cheer the heart,
And, for the nonce, fresh strength impart.
But, can we live them out in life,
Amid the worry and the strife
That cross our path, and passive be,
When failure or success we see ?

Can HEART and WILL be satisfied,
When longed-for fruit has been denied ?
Can anxious thoughts be thrust aside,
And inward rest and calm abide,
When our most cherished hopes have failed,
And when by Doubt we are assailed ?
This I would know : Has mortal man
Built up his life upon such plan ?
Have you this teaching tested, tried,
And found your hopes all gratified ?

No, Lily, not " ALL GRATIFIED ;"
My fondest hopes are oft denied ;
But still I say, " THY WILL BE DONE ;"
And thus grand victories I've won.
To yield submissive to God's will,
And see Him aye in us fulfil
His pleasure, brings to heart and mind
Most glorious peace, so that we find
New JOY in service, and new POWER
Encompassing us every hour.
But, lo ! our ALL must yielded be,
If we from CARE would aye be free.
And not alone our WILL and WAY,
But all our WORK from day to day.

In CONSECRATION we had thought
That ALL was to the ALTAR brought :

Our will was one with Jesus' will ;
We gladly wished him to fulfil
In us His purposes and plans ;
We joyed to think that His eye scans
Our inmost thoughts and each desire ;
We felt the glow of Heaven's fire
Refining, filling, giving rest,
And making us supremely blest.
The will was wholly sanctified ;
To self we had entirely died ;
We did His will with glad delight,
And walked well-pleasing in His sight.
To Him we did commit our WAY,
In loving, humble trust each day,
To follow Him where'er He led ;
And path of loving service tread.
Or, if to suffering and pain
He called us, still we did retain
Our inward rest and cheerly said :
' How toothsome is Affliction's bread !'

But CONSECRATION here took end ;
Our WORK and SERVICE did impend
Upon ourselves ; and ANXIOUS CARE,
With all its worry and its wear,
Was searching for the ripened fruit
Before the seed had taken root.

Lo ! we forgot our WORK to lay
Upon the ALTAR, day by day,—
To leave ALL in our Father's hands;
And, patient, wait till He commands
The sharpened sickle to uptake
And reap our harvest. For our sake
He must, if CARE doth in us lurk,
'Let Patience have her perfect work.'

Leander, prithee, may I ask
If *you* have taken up this task,
And in your work have banished care,
And conquered worry and its wear ?
I long to see such triumph won—
See how the Victor's race is run.

Lo ! Lily, in my first essày
At public service—well the day
Do I remember—I had CARE:
In toil myself I did not spare;
My joy in service knew no bound;
In saving precious souls I found
Supreme delight; each day and night
I preached and pleaded, till the light
Of Heav'n would dawn on some sad soul—
Till Sin's huge burden off would roll.

'Twas such a grand Revival scene,
As cheers not hearts of all, I ween,

Who labour lovingly for men
To bring them back to God again.
While many entered into light,
Lo! others lay in deepest night;
They longed for PEACE, they strove and prayed,
Each day beseeching heavenly aid;
But still no PEACE—no REST within—
No freedom from the load of sin.
O'er such sad souls I daily yearned,—
I had not yet the secret learned
Of casting on the Christ my care,—
My nights I spent in wrestling prayer
That wisdom might to me be given
To lift up souls, by anguish riven,
And set them free from their sad plight
To bask in the Eternal Light.

The burden of my daily work
Was joy; no duty would I shirk—
For I with love and zeal o'erflowed—
And daily I would bear the load
Of anxious, loving, thoughtful care
For souls distressed—their sorrows share.

In this I erred; I should have laid
On Christ my burden; by His aid
I might have triumphed over CARE—
Have said: 'No WORRY AND NO WEAR'

Shall be my motto. Day by day
Our WORK may on the ALTAR lay.

But, hark! Leander; you say "may"—
"Our WORK *may* on the ALTAR lay."
'Tis this my longing heart would know :
Has your experience proved it so ?
Have you in service been set free
From anxious care ? Did worry flee
Before your faith, like fleeting cloud
Before the wind ; and did the crowd
Of carking cares no lodgment find
Within your calm and restful mind ?
Can we live out in daily life
This teaching, and be free from strife ?

Lo! Lily, I had tried to say
That this was but my first essày
At Christian work. In after days—
To God in Christ be all the praise—
A higher note I struck, and paid
To God high honour; ALL I laid
Upon the ALTAR—WORK, and WILL,
And WAY—and there, lo! they are still.

The scene is changed; the seas I crossed;
I went to seek and save the lost—
In Northern Britain's northmost isle
I sought by service to beguile
The summer months that lay between
The College sessions.   There, I ween,
The Lord did lead; for I did leave
My web of life for Him to weave.
At His disposal I had placed
My time, my service.

     Those who faced
The rigour of this northern clime
Were hardly fishermen.   No crime,
Nor " drink," nor language foul, I found
Upon the island; and no sound
Of Folly's revelry was there :
Lo ! life was sober, serious, fair.
The dangers of their calling made
Them grave and earnest.   They obeyed
The high commands of God Most High;
And daily felt His presence nigh.

These earnest souls I went to teach
The WAY OF HOLINESS—to preach
A full salvation—perfect peace—
And from Sin's power complete release.
My message was with joy received,
And many on the Lord believed

F

For PARDON, PEACE, and HOLINESS,
And POWER other souls to bless.
For weeks and months the work went on,—
For Light from Heav'n had on us shone,—
Each night I taught, or preached the Word;
And every night some heart was stirred
To seek a closer walk, a higher life,
And freedom from all inward strife.
Inquirers lingered long behind,
All yearning for that peace of mind,
Which they were told the Lord would give
To those, who yielded ALL to live
Pure, consecrated, Christian lives.
To give this PEACE the Spirit strives
Within the heart, until the soul,
In glad surrender, yields the whole
Of mortal being—THOUGHT, and WILL,
And HEART—to God, that He may fill,
With His own fulness, every part,
And sanctify both mind and heart.
With hundreds face to face I spoke;
I sought to break the galling yoke
Of sin and wilfulness that crushed
Their weary souls, and quenched or hushed
The Spirit's voice within.   There came
To many heavenly fire and flame;
The heart was sanctified and filled
With peace, till all within was stilled.

The life was gentle, pure, and bright;
The face all radiant as the light;
They gladly witnessed to the dower
Of heavenly grace, and proved its power.

But, lo! a few sad, sullen souls,
Convicted, feeling burning coals
Of fiery wrath upon them poured,
With proud self-will within them stored,
Resisted long, before they came
And sought release in Jesus' Name.
With these I wrestled; for them prayed,
Invoking Heav'n's supremest aid;
And patiently I sought to win
Them from the love of self and sin.

In former days I would have CARE—
Would, sleepless, spend whole nights in prayer,
If burdened souls, like these, were laid
Upon my heart.   But now I played
The part of one, whose faith can rise
Triumphant through the clouded skies,
And see God's Hand in long delays;
And trust Him in His strangest ways.
I said, "My Father, let Thy Will
"In them be done; from seeming ill
"Thou aye the greatest good canst bring;
"And these crushed hearts one day shall sing,

"And praise Thee for the lingering way
"Which led them to Eternal Day."
And it was so. For one by one
God's mighty work in them was done:
They yielded to the Spirit's call,
And gladly, promptly, laid their ALL
Upon God's ALTAR.   All a-fire
With love and zeal, they tuned their lyre
In loudest notes the Lord to praise
For seeming lingering delays.
With grateful hearts they testified
That LOVE OF SELF and WILFUL PRIDE—
From which they oft had sought release—
By their long, anxious quest for peace
Had been o'ercome.   They each confessed
That these delays for them were best.
And thus, according to my prayer,
I saw there was no room for CARE.

But say, Leander, did you feel
No anxious thoughts and troubles steal
Across your mind by night or day,
While on sad souls such burdens lay?

No, Lily, I was not aware
Of slightest anxious thought or care.
Throughout these months my inward rest
Was perfect.   Not a care distressed

My peaceful soul, or day or night.
I longed to see the glorious light
Of Heav'n illume each dark sad heart,
And perfect peace to all impart;
But I had learned that God knows best
The way to lead sad souls to rest,—
The time to speak peace to the soul—
To say, "Thy faith hath made thee whole."
He times events by His sweet will;
And they His purposes fulfil:
His purposes, so good and wise,
Should aye be pleasing in our eyes.

He who enjoys this Rest of Faith,
Each day yields ALL to God, and saith:
"Thy will in me be done; me use
"As in Thy wisdom Thou dost choose;
"Guide me in service, how and where
"To speak Thy message; I will dare
"To leave with Thee the time of fruit;
"Thy wisdom I will not dispute."

Lo! Lily, this the simple test,
'TIS PERFECT TRUST GIVES PERFECT REST.
"Trust thou in God, be doing good,
"And verily thou shalt have food;
"Delight thyself in God, and He
"Thy heart's desire will give to thee;

" Commit to God thy way, thy Light
" Shall shine, and all thy path make bright;
" Be hushed 'fore God, and, patient, wait,
" And fret not, if the fruit seem late."
Good David knew the steps of Faith,
And walked in them; for, lo! he saith :
Fret not, but TRUST, DELIGHT, COMMIT;
They take these steps who humbly sit
At Jesus' feet, and seek to know
Naught but His Will, and daily grow
More like the perfect Pattern Life,
That ne'er was marred by inward strife.

Leander, is it wrong to fret,
When pathway oft seems strangely set
With thorns and briars,—when we see
No fruit of labour ? Can it be,
That failure shall no pangs impart,
Nor rive the earnest, tender heart ?

Lo ! Lily, we're not worms of dust ;
There is no failure, where there's trust ;
Our Faith should every murmur rout ;
For where there's murmuring there is doubt.
Distrust and Doubt are bosom friends,
And weaken man for all high ends ;
But Faith may rise in all her might,
And doubt and fretting put to flight.

If Christ be real to us, and near,
We'll rise above each fretting fear;
We will not murmur, chafe, and weep;
From all distrust the Lord will keep.
Yea, rest and calm *must* dwell within;
For worry is akin to sin.

Leander, I can never rest,
Until I know that I am blest,
With this great gift of " perfect PEACE,"
And from all worry get release.
I'll pray and wrestle, struggle, strive,
And daily keep my faith alive
By loving, kindly, helpful deeds—
By ministering to human needs.
I'll try impatience to repress,
And God, perchance, will deign to bless.

But, Lily, do not toil and strive
By effort Faith to keep alive;
Lo! Faith is stillness, quiet, rest;
Be passive, if you would be blest.
Let Jesus come in all His grace,
And make your heart His dwelling-place.
He is our PEACE; when He doth fill
The trusting heart, it must be still.

To unfilled harbour comes the tide,
With dash and splash on every side;

And there is turmoil till it's filled,—
Then one great ripple—all is stilled.
So with the HEART in Christian life ;
While filling, there is turmoil, strife :
Let it be filled,—then, all is PEACE—
From care and worry sweet release.

Lo ! Israel, whom Joshua led
To Jordan's banks on manna fed,
Were drawing near the Promised Land—
The Land of Rest.   By God's command
Themselves they sanctified ; for, lo!
The Holy only o'er may go.
Between them and their " land of gold "
Great Jordan's waters proudly rolled.
And now to Faith there comes a test,
Ere God can give the Land of Rest.
Their rest must be the Rest of Faith ;
Hence to the Priests Jehovah saith :
" When ye are come to Jordan's brink—
" Let not faint heart within you sink,—
" Ye all in Jordan STILL must stand,
" A brave, devoted, fearless band.
" To Abraham's Faith this Land I gave ;
" And now Faith's feet must press the wave
" Of brimming Jordan, ere he rolls
" His waters back ; your trusting souls

" Must show the Courage and the Rest
" That flow from Faith.   Lo ! this the test
" Of fitness to perform My Will :
" In midst of Jordan stand ye still."

    The faithful Priests with manly tread
The crossing of the Jordan led ;
Their Faith for them must make a road,
For Jordan all his banks o'erflowed ;
But, ere they touch with lifted feet
The brimming waters, as was meet,
Proud Jordan halts, and hastes away :
Its triumphs Faith displayed that day.

    In midst of Jordan on dry ground,
The Priests that bear the ark are found ;
By stillness they their strength do show :
They fear not Jordan's threat'ning flow.
They stood in Jordan still, 'tis said,
Till all the people whom they led,
By God's command had clean passed o'er,
And all were safe on Canaan's shore.

    This stillness is the Rest of Faith.
To us our Joshua—Jesus—saith :
" Be still, and know that I am God ;
" Your Jordan may be deep and broad ;

" Its waters may its banks o'erflow,
" Ev'n all the HARVEST-TIME; but know
" That faith is strong to do and dare,
" And free.the soul from anxious care."

Leander, this is Faith indeed—
To go where'er our God may lead;
To let Him take us by the hand,
And bring us to "the goodly land"—
The Land of Rest where all is still—
No inward strife—no ruffled will.
My life was wrong through all these years;
'Twas lack of faith brought fretting fears.
I was not passive, quiet, still;
But wrestled, bustled, set my will
To conquer, as if strength were mine,
Instead of seeking strength Divine.
Lo! now in STILLNESS I will find
The REST of FAITH and POWER combined.
How glorious is this view of life!—
No failure, worry, care, nor strife!

Yes, free from failure in the life;
And free from care and inward strife.
But, Lily, outward strife you'll meet,
Until your triumphs are complete.
God's people in the Land of Rest
Had foes to fight. God saw 'twas best

That *they* should drive the nations out,
And, by His aid, all en'mies rout.

' These Seven Nations represent
The evil forces yet unspent,
Which all, within the land, must face:
These we must conquer by the grace
And power of God. 'Twas good that they
By their own hand those foes should slay.
Resistance showed their ill intent,
More than if they adrift were sent
By God in some mysterious way,
Or conquered in a single day.
These Nations thus were foes declared;
Their friendship never could be shared;
God's Israel must ever be
From such kept separate and free.
So, Lily, it is good for those,
Who would be free from wily foes,
To meet them in the open plain,
Decisive vict'ry there to gain.
The fight will be the Fight of Faith;
To Joshua, and to us, God saith:
" The Lord shall fight for you; be still,
" And let Him work in you His Will."
We consecrate ourselves for War;
Then Faith mounts the triumphal car;

We let the Lord our en'mies rout;
And, standing still, we vict'ry shout.

For Seven Years this Holy War
Was waged in Canaan. Not a scar,
Nor wound, nor loss, nor pain was felt—
No timid heart with fear did melt,—
Except through Achan's wilful sin,
When God did glorious vict'ry win
At Jericho. His selfish greed
There led him on to traitorous deed;
And, full of lust, his hand he soils.
That wedge of gold and all the spoils
Were God's—firstfruits of victory—
An off'ring for His treasury,
'Twas God he robbed—a heinous sin;—
No more can Israel vict'ry win
Till sin is purged. So Achan dies
By God's command in cursed guise.
And thus God taught that, to be blest
With vict'ry in the Land of Rest,
We must be kept from wilful sin—
Be purged from SELF—be pure within.

LEANDER, I have tried to claim
Release from sin in Jesus' Name.
May we not from the LOVE and POWER
Of SIN be freed by heavenly dower

Of Holy Ghost? Can God not KEEP,
That fruit of sin we shall not reap,
Because Sin's seed we do not sow,
And like the Christ help us to grow?
If God is KEEPER, HELPER, FRIEND,
And we to His Will our wills bend,
Why should our service failure show?
Why should not life be all aglow
With LOVE and JOY and PERFECT PEACE,
And every inward struggle cease?

Since I in STILLNESS found sweet rest,
In service I am doubly blest,
His service now is pure delight;
I live each moment in His sight;
I feel His Presence ever near;
I know no failure and no fear.
I say, "Lord, I am but a child;
"Like Jesus, keep me undefiled!
"As Thou hast saved me by Thy grace,
"Aye make my heart Thy dwelling-place!
"I with Thy fulness would be filled,
"And have the waves of trouble stilled!
"I'll tread the path which Thou dost choose;
"If Thou in service canst me use,
"I give myself, my time, my ALL,
"Each moment waiting for Thy call."

Lo! in this Rest of Faith I've found
Such joy and glory all around,
That every spot seems holy ground,
And Earth's harsh notes have all sweet sound.
I see God's purpose everywhere;
I have no worry and no care;
I sow in faith, and, patient, wait;
On failure never calculate.
His Spirit, "as a voice behind,"
Aye helps me the right path to find,
And daily witnesseth within
That I am kept from conscious sin,
Like Paul, " to me to live is Christ,"
And life is now imparadised.

Yes, Lily, to be with the Christ
Is to have life imparadised.
Our Heaven on Earth may be begun
If by His strength Life's race is run.
Good Enoch, in the olden time,
Walked with His God—a life sublime;
To him was testimony given
That God he pleased; lo! this was heaven.
Of Caleb, too, Jephunneh's son,
And Joshua, the son of Nun,
The Holy History declares
That they knew naught of carking cares,

Or fear, or failure in the life,
Though sore beset by outward strife;
They wholly followed God's command,
And, scatheless, settled in the Land.
Not once, in all those forty years,
Did Faith give place to doubts and fears.
They yielded ALL—desire and will—
To God; and He their life did fill
With His own fulness, giving Power
And perfect Peace—Heav'n's noblest dower.

Lo! Paul lived out this LIFE OF FAITH;
He tells experience when he saith:
" Now unto God be thanks and praise:
" Who causeth us in all our ways
" To triumph in His Son, the Christ;"
His life was thus imparadised.
" With Christ, my Lord, I'm crucified;
" To SELF and SIN, I Paul, have died;
" And I no longer live, but Christ
"Doth live in me. With Him my tryst
" I daily keep. This earthly life—
" Although around me sin is rife—
" I live in faith through God's dear Son:
"In Him my triumphs all are won."
The greatest hero of his time,
'Twas Christ that made his life sublime;

Apart from Christ he aye was weak ;
Lo! these the words we hear him speak :
" By loss of all things I am blest,
" If Christly Power but on me rest."
His strength he found in Christ alone,
Hence fear and failure were unknown.
The towering heights of Faith he climbed ;
The bells of Heaven sweet music chimed ;
In glorious ecstasy he saw
The highest Heaven ; filled with awe,
He paused before the glorious sight,
Enraptured by the heavenly light.
Lo! from that day he walked with God ;
The path of HOLINESS he trod.

His first prayer proved his heart was true :
" LORD, WHAT WILT THOU HAVE ME TO DO ? "
To do God's will his one desire ;
To this one note he tuned his lyre.
How rough soe'er the path he trod,
He knew that he was led by God ;
In life or death, in peace or war,
In all things more than conqueror.

Leander, ere I knew this REST—
This PEACE and POWER, with which I'm blest—
I thought the glowing stories told
Of those devoted men of old

Were not for us.   Lives so sublime
Seemed far beyond what, in our time,
We could expect of mortal man.
I thought God had a *special* plan
And purpose in their lives; but now
I feel that if, like them, we bow
In all things to the will of Christ,
OUR LIVES may be imparadised.
Like them, no failure we need know,
If, in God's strength, we forward go
To every duty.   If each day
In all we do, in all we say,
We wholly follow God's command,
We are within the Promised Land.
To me it is a Land of Rest;
Each day with perfect Peace I'm blest;
My heart o'erflows with gladdening song;
And holy Joy makes weakness strong.

Lo, Lily, Strength will aye abound;
For Life's grand secret you have found.
To this we all must come at length:
" JOY IN THE LORD OUR ONLY STRENGTH."
In STILLNESS and in JOY we find
True food, and best, for heart and mind;
For fellowship with God in Christ
Bestows upon us strength unpriced.

G

Henceforth with POWER you will speak;
No more will you call Woman WEAK.
Not in ourselves are Strength and Power;
They come to us as Heaven's dower.

The LIFE OF FAITH is more than REST,
Lo! 'tis a life that's doubly blest;
The REST twin sister is to POWER;
The last the Fruit, the first the Flower.
Where Tree of Faith has taken root,
There aye will be both Flower and Fruit.

Lo, Lily, Rest and Joy within
Prove you are kept from conscious sin.
With Purity the Christ will dwell;
So that in Power you shall excel.
The Christ abides in trustful heart,
And POWER and PEACE need ne'er depart.

Leander, these are words of cheer;
Henceforward I will banish fear.
It seemed to me too much to claim,
Ev'n in the all-prevailing Name,
That PEACE and POWER should aye abide;
But, if each moment God will guide
And keep and strengthen, lo! we may
Live holy lives from day to day:
This precious truth, "THE LORD WILL KEEP,"
Rich harvest gives for Faith to reap.

Lo! I have had sweet foretaste given
Of gracious POWER, as late I've striven
To lead poor wanderers to the Christ.
I spoke of Jesus sacrificed
·For sins of men; of His great love
In coming from His home above
To live on earth, and die for men
To lift man up to God again.
As I the touching story told,
In words as simple as they're old,
The strongest bowed, and deeply felt
The Power of God; their hearts did melt
And overflow in sobs and tears.
Most glorious was the sight! One fears
To speak of such transcendent scene;
'Twould seem, to even ears most keen
And sensitive to heavenly things,
Like airy flights on Fancy's wings.
The Power was not in me, I know,
To touch, and rouse, and quick subdue
Strong hearts in manner so sublime,
For selfsame words in former time
Fell powerless on selfsame hearts;
But now they come like piercing darts,
Or like the light'ning's flash and thrill,—
So quick do they subdue the will.
And, lo! these men of spotted life,
Who loved the haunts where sin is rife,

Are quickly changed in life and loves.
Ta'en from among the pots,* like doves
With white-plumed wings they now appear—
Pure, bright, and full of godly cheer.

Yes, Lily, though "a woman weak,"
God clothes with Power the words you speak.
Through quiet, restful, trusting heart
Alone can God rich grace impart.
Nor man nor woman can be strong
To fight with and cast out the wrong,
That dwells within the human heart,
By skilful tact and subtle art.
There is no power, but POWER DIVINE,
Can touch, ennoble, and refine
Perverted natures, steeped in sin,
And cleanse the life without, within.
This precious truth you now have proved:
You know 'twas GOD Who these hearts moved.

Leander, now the truth I know:
All Strength and Power from God do flow;
We are but empty vessels all,—
No matter whether great or small.
When with God's fulness I was filled,
Lo! every anxious fear was stilled;
With inward REST came glorious POWER—
Most precious Fruit from Faith's fair Flower.

---

* PSALM lxviii. 13.

When erst for Christ I sought to speak,
I thought my WOMANHOOD was weak;
But, lo! 'twas faith in God I lacked:
I trusted to my skill and tact—
To love, devotion, pity, zeal,—
To earnest, touching, strong appeal.
Alas! my words all fruitless fell—
My anguish tongue can never tell;
For Gloom's dark torrents on me rushed,
And fell Despair my heart had crushed.
But life is now a calm, deep sea,
From storms and waves of trouble free.
Life seems to be one great long prayer,
Unbroken by distracting care.

This Rest of Faith brings glorious dower,
And simplest words are clothed with POWER.
My tongue has caught the ALTAR-FIRE;
I speak and plead, and never tire;
And anxious souls, borne down with grief,
In Jesus Christ get sweet relief.
And, lo! my pen seems dipped in flame;
Each day I write, in Jesus' Name,
To friends I loved in former days;
And many hearts are filled with praise,
That God some word should give to me
To lead their thoughts to Calvary.

O that the wide world could but know
The joys unspeakable that flow
From fellowship with God in Christ—
'Twould then become imparadised.

Yes, Lily, men must know and feel
That Christ's Religion is most real.
To save men from sin's power and strife
We must live out in daily life,
Before men's eyes, the truths we teach,
Else we will fail sad hearts to reach.
We must live consecrated lives;
And Christian Churches must be hives
Of loving, self-denying toil,
If they would gather precious spoil
From fields by en'my occupied.
All LOVE OF SELF must be denied,—
ALL PRIDE, and LUXURY, and EASE,
And things the carnal mind that please.

When on God's ALTAR we lay all,
We must not think our offering small—
Too small for God to use and bless;
In God's Hand talents, more or less,
Avail not.   He doth crown with POWER
The feeblest, humblest, by the dower
Of the Almighty Holy Ghost,
And makes of one a mighty host.

Too long was Woman reckoned WEAK;
Too long denied her right to speak
In mixed assembly.   She must take
Her rightful place with man, and make
Her presence and her power felt
In Christian work, till hearts shall melt
Beneath her tenderness and love,
And words inspired by Heavenly Dove.

You have a mission, and you must,
In love to man and humble trust
In God, go forth in Jesus' Name,
And lovingly to all proclaim
This REST OF FAITH—a glorious PEACE,
Which from all care gives sweet release,
Which POWER in service aye bestows,—
Till deserts blossom as the rose.

You must urge all to consecrate
Their life—their talents, small and great,—
To Christian service.   Tell each one
That, while this earthly race they run,
God has a work for each to do:
" THE HARVEST'S GREAT, THE LABOURERS FEW."
Both men and women, one and all,
Who have been rescued from sin's thrall,
With first Love's glowing ardour thrilled,
With bright enthusiasm filled,

Must rush into the thickest fight,
And tell sad souls from what sad plight
The grace of God delivered them,—
How Strength Divine helped them to stem
The rushing tide of SELF and SIN,
And gave a glorious PEACE within.
Thus men will learn that they may win
Deliverance from the love of sin,
And from its power, ev'n here and now,
If humbly they to Jesus bow.

'Tis needful that the world should know
That highest happiness doth flow
From true Religion IN THIS LIFE,
With all its worry and its strife.
By happy heart and radiant face
And lives ennobled by God's grace,
We prove to men that Christ doth give
Most gracious power to those who live
In constant fellowship with Him;
So that Joy's lamp will ne'er burn dim.
Lo! sad, benighted souls must see,
In our bright lives, that Christ sets free
From care and worry all who trust
His LOVE and POWER; hence we must
Upon all Christian men impress
The crying need of HOLINESS.

'Tis consecrated lives alone
That sin and passion can dethrone
From place and power in human hearts:
Not purest doctrine, nor the arts
Of skilful teaching can impress
The careless, and find quick access
To hearts inured to vice and sin:
'Tis Christlike lives that best can win
Such souls for God; and let them see
What Christ has done to set them free.
Lo! "OTHER CHRISTS" we all must be,
If we would cope with misery.
We must have earnest Christian men—
And women in their thousands ten,
In beautiful and modest guise,—
Aye living out before men's eyes
A happy, pure, triumphant life
Amid the haunts of sin and strife:
For, not till then, will men believe
That mortals can from Christ receive
Sufficient power to break with sin,
And crush its reigning power within.

Such helps to faith the fallen need:
There's naught like Christly lives to plead
With sinful, sin-sick souls, and prove
That God is EVERLASTING LOVE.

" Holiness to the Lord."
Exodus xxviii., 36.

" Who is Like Thee in Holiness ? "
Exodus xv., 11.

" Perfecting Holiness in the Fear of God."
2. Cor. vii., 1.

" Without Holiness no Man Shall see the Lord."
Hebrews xii., 14.

" Her Merchandise and her hire shall be
HOLINESS TO THE LORD."
Isaiah xxiii., 18.

HYMNS

on

Scripture Texts and Themes,

and on

HOLINESS AND CONSECRATION.

—:◇:—

LIGHTS AND SHADOWS IN LIFE.

" And now men see not the bright light that is in the clouds;
but the wind passeth and cleanseth them."—Job xxxvii. 21.

1 There are clouds on the mountain side,
    As we climb to serener air;
But we pierce them, as upward we glide;
    Then we bask in the sunlight fair.
For above the dark cloud is the sun,
    There shining in glory and strength;
And all who the summit have won
    Find the light and the shining at length.

2 To those in the valley below
    There is naught to be seen but the cloud;
But on yonder hillside there's a bow,
    Never seen by the thoughtless crowd:
And that bow is a harbinger fair,
    That points to bright skies above;
For it tells us the sun is still there
    Fulfilling his mission of love.

3 The dark angry clouds he'll dispel,
    As he pours forth his glorious rays;
And he'll light up each vale and dell,
    And brighten the gloomiest days.
Though the fast-fleeting clouds have obscured
    For a time the bright rays of the sun;
Yet for aye the light has endured,
    And the shining the victory has won.

4 Lo! here is a picture of life,
    With its varying shadow and light:
Some have cloud and worry and strife,
    And grope in the darkness of night:
But others have pierced through the clouds,
    And are breathing the mountain air,—
Far up 'bove the herding crowds,—
    Where only the holy dare.

5 Ah! these have seen the bright light
    That is in the dark cloud o'erhead;
For they've learned to fight the good fight,
    By the Captain of God's host led.
They have met the arch-tempter full oft;
    He has chased them over the plain;
But for help to the hills aloft
    They have turned, and never in vain.

6 We once had our doubts and our fears,—
　　All darkness and cloud within,—
All gloom, perplexity, tears,—
　　Though hated was every sin.
We saw not the light in the cloud,
　　Although it was shining behind;
We groped, and we prayed, and we vowed,
　　But no light nor rest could we find.

7 We were puzzled, perplexed, distressed,
　　And we knew not where to turn;
Our anguished souls were oppressed,
　　And our hearts as with fire did burn,
The heavens above were as brass;
　　Our pleadings and cries were in vain,—
Will the dark cloud never o'erpass?
　　Will the sun never shine again?

8 Ah! ye clouds, will ye burst and outpour
　　Your fiercest vials of wrath?—
All at once let it come and be o'er,
　　That the sunshine may brighten my path!
For this darkness is awful and dread—
　　A thick darkness that may be felt
All around, within, and o'erhead,—
　　Heart, crushed and ready to melt.

9 Sad soul, why linger ye there
　　In darkness that chills and that kills;
Lo! yonder the sunlight fair,
　　Makes glorious all the hills!
Up, up and away to the light;
　　It is Jesus that's shining for thee!
For all it is equally bright;
　　For all it is perfectly free.

10 But the light is for those who come—
　　For those who believe in its shining:
Of hearts' troubles this is the sum,—
　　They choose to go on in repining;
They elect to sit under the cloud;
　　They hug their doubts and their fears;
They bear their own burdens, though bowed;
　　They cherish their fretting and tears.

11 You must go where the sun is shining,
　　And enjoy the comforting light;
You must hush your heart's sad repining,
　　And come out from the gloom of your night.
The sun still shines in the heaven;
　　On earth it brightens some spot;
To you and to me it is given
　　To seek the bright light—is it not?

12 You must see the wind cleansing the cloud,
    Dispersing its blackness and gloom;
You must—all awed and bowed—
    In your heart for God's Spirit make room.
God's Spirit alone can give light
    To your soul in the darkness of doubt;
God's Spirit alone can give might;
    And all your enemies rout.

13 If on Jesus your burdens you lay,
    He will lovingly bear them with you;
He will help and comfort each day,
    And each night your strength will renew.
His own cross—our cross—one sad day,
    He dragged till He fell, it would seem;
On " one Simon " the lighter end lay,
    But Jesus still bore the cross-beam.

14 And still of our heaviest crosses
    He bears the heavier end;
And, in all our griefs and losses,
    A kind helping hand He doth lend.
He *still* shares our sorrows and tears;
    He still *weeps* with the mourning band,
And *still* his sympathy cheers
    Lone hearts in every land.

H

15　Why, then, at the clouds take alarm?
　　　They come but to send you to Him;
　　The darkness and thunder can't harm
　　　If the eye of faith grow not dim.
　　Faith's *eye* sees *every* cloud riven;
　　　And behind sees " the silver lining;"
　　Faith can see, far off in the heaven,
　　　The Sun of Righteousness shining.

16　As the cloud is cleansed by the wind,
　　　And the shining sun in his might;
　　So the *good* Spirit, dwelling within,
　　　Will cleanse you and make you bright.
　　Still, Lord, there'll be shadow and light
　　　In the lot of Thy children here;
　　But every cloud will be bright,
　　　As we love Thee, and feel Thee near.

SOUL-LONGINGS.

TUNE: AUSTRIA.

1 Oh! my soul is longing, longing,
   To be resting in Thy Love;
   Longing for the joy unending
   In the realms of light above.

2 Oh! my soul is longing, longing,
   For the riches of Thy Grace;
   For the glorious heaven-lit beaming
   Of the Sun of Righteousness.

3 Oh! my soul is longing, longing,
   For a stronger, mightier Faith:
   For a heart to grasp each promise,
   And to rest on, "Jesus saith."

4 Oh! my soul is longing, longing,
   Saviour, for Thy perfect Peace:
   For the stillness Thou hast promised;
   For the joys that never cease.

5 Oh! my soul is longing, longing,
   For the sweet light of Thy Face;
   For the comfort and the keeping
   Of Thine all-embracing grace.

6 Oh! my soul is longing, longing,
    To be clothed with Power Divine;
To be filled with Thine own fulness,—
    Thou hast promised, Saviour mine.

7 Oh! my soul is longing, longing,
    Lord, to be entirely Thine,—
Thine this moment, Thine forever,—
    That for Jesus I may shine.

8 Oh! my soul is longing, longing,
    To be filled with Holy Fire;
To take up my Master's mantle—
    Serve from love, and not for hire.

9 Oh! my soul is longing, longing,
    For the coming of The King.
O to see Him in His Kingdom!
    O what joy that day will bring!

10 Then Thou'lt satisfy my longing;
    There Thou'lt fill me with Thy Love;
There my joy will know no ending
    In my glorious Home above.

STEP BY STEP WITH JESUS.

TUNE: KIRKBRADDAN, OR, LYNDHURST.

1 STEP by step with Jesus:
  Trusting in His grace;
  He the chief of sinners
  Clasps in His embrace.

2 Step by step with Jesus:
  Crucified to sin;
  Made, by blood most precious,
  White as snow within.

3 Step by step with Jesus
  In the narrow way;
  He, my Friend and Helper,
  Guides me day by day.

4 Step by step with Jesus:
  Doing God's sweet will;
  He, my King and Keeper,
  Rules the billows still.

5 Step by step with Jesus:
  Walking in the Light;
  Following in His footsteps
  Makes my pathway bright.

6 Step by step with Jesus:
   Filled with His own PEACE;
   Conscious of His PRESENCE.
   Joy knows no surcease.

7 Step by step with Jesus:
   Seeking out the lost,—
   Toiling, pleading, saving,—
   Counting not the cost.

8 Step by step with Jesus:
   Strengthened by His might;
   Strong to fight His battles;
   Conquering in the fight.

9 Step by step with Jesus:
   All of self subdued;
   He my Great Exemplar,—
   With His love imbued.

10 Step by step with Jesus:
   By His Spirit filled;
   Every passion conquered;
   Every murmur stilled.

11 Step by step with Jesus
　　Into trouble's sea ;
　He, my loving Comforter,
　　Bears it all in me.

12 Step by step with Jesus :
　　Kept from wilful sin ;
　Like the King's own daughter,
　　" Glorious within."

13 Step by step with Jesus :
　　Touched with Heaven's Fire ;
　Tongue and lips His praises
　　Speak and never tire.

14 Step by step with Jesus :
　　Shining for my King ;
　Life, and look, and labours,
　　All His praises bring.

15 Step by step with Jesus :
　　Resting in His love ;
　Happy in His service
　　As the saints above.

16 Step by step with Jesus :
    Clothed with heav'nly POWER ;
Safe from wiles of tempter,—
    Safe in my " Strong tower."

17 Step by step with Jesus
    'Midst the waves of grief ;
Night may have its weeping,—
    Morn will bring relief.

18 Step by step with Jesus :
    Sharing others' tears ;
Weeping with the weeper,
    Banishing their fears.

19 Step by step with Jesus
    Till the end shall come ;
Watching for His coming—
    Longing to go home.

20 Step by step with Jesus
    To my home above ;
The crown of life receiving ;
    Dwelling in His Love.

CONSECRATION.

" Sanctify yourselves, for to-morrow the Lord will do wonders among you.—Josu. iii. 5.

By Jordan's banks the people stand,
Their eye upon the promised land ;
Before they enter into rest
Their faith and love the Lord will test.
The rest must be the Rest of Faith ;
Hence by command their leader saith :
" Now Consecrate yourselves anew ;
" To-morrow God will wonders do."

Between them and the goodly land
Proud Jordan's waves roll high and grand ;
And while they wait with wondering eyes,
They see the flood still higher rise ;
Why, therefore, should there be delay—
Why should their cautious leader say :
" Now consecrate yourselves anew ;
To-morrow God will wonders do."

Impatience would have hasted o'er,
Have rashly sought the further shore ;
Would chafe and murmur at delay :
" Why wait and lose another day ? "
But, lo ! the leader's patient faith
Obeys the Lord ; he calmly saith :
" Come, consecrate yourselves anew ;
" To-morrow God will wonders do."

Is day of Consecration lost
With Jordan's flowing stream uncrossed ?
Ah ! no ; our loving Lord knows best
The time to bring us into rest ;
Until we wholly break with sin,
God cannot give us peace within :
" Come, consecrate yourselves anew ;
" To-morrow God will wonders do."

Were days of Consecration lost—
Lo ! forty days at Pentecost—
When Faith lay waiting, calm and still,
For God His promise to fulfil ?
See thousands claiming Christ as Lord,
While John and Peter preach the Word :
" Yes, consecrate yourselves anew ;
" To-morrow God will wonders do."

And still the same old word holds true :
If God for us great things will do,
We aye must wait and patient lie
For power and blessing from on high ;
In all our work obedient faith
Must hearken to the word which saith :
"Come, consecrate yourselves anew ;
"To-morrow God will wonders do."

Lo ! on the morrow comes the power ;
First, Consecration ; then, the dower
Of blessing and of heavenly might,
Lo ! filling all the soul with light ;
Bestowing love and pure desire,
And touching lips with holy fire :
"Come, consecrate yourselves anew ;
"To-morrow God will wonders do."

Lord, help Thy trusting children all
To hearken to Thy gracious call,
And daily live in holy mood,
Aye finding joy in doing good,
That there may be no long delays,—
No waiting months, or weeks, or days :
"Now consecrate yourselves anew ;
"To-morrow God will wonders do."

TO LIVE IS CHRIST.

"To me to live is Christ."—PHIL. i. 21.

"To live is Christ"—O wondrous word!
   "To me to live is Christ"!
What noble aspiration stirred
   Great Paul to keep his tryst!
He lived as one no longer free
   To call himself his own;
He sought no higher liberty
   Than to be Christ's alone.

"To me to live is Christ"!—brave man,
   Can mortal man say this?
Is there a life on earth that can
   Thus claim to be like His?
"To me to live is Christ,"—ah, yes,
   This thy ideal high,—
To live like Him, and others bless,—
   For men to live and die.

O noble saint! O hero brave!
    What change in thee is wrought!
Time was when thou at Christ didst rave,
    And fiercely 'gainst Him fought.
What hast thou seen in Him, O Paul,
    To cool thy furious rage?
'Twas something more than comes to all—
    The sobering of age.

Ah, yes, I saw Him on the way,
    As face to face we met;
And ne'er before was such a day,
    Nor man so sore beset.
His face ten thousand suns outshone,
    His raiment white as light;
My spark of life was almost gone,
    So glorious was the sight.

He spoke in tones that made me bow—
    So gentle, so divine,—
"SAUL, SAUL, WHY PERSECUTEST THOU,"—
    And pierced this heart of mine.
The words, like light'ning, thrilled me through;
    New creature I became;
No tongue may tell what then I knew—
    His power proud hearts to tame.

Instinctively my wistful heart
   Cried out, " Lord, who art Thou " ?
Quick came the word—divinest art !—
   " I'm Jesus, to Me bow."
My will, no longer ruled by pride,
   Submissive, yielded all :
" Lord, I am Thine, whate'er betide,
   With Thee to stand or fall."

My heart was filled with wondrous peace,
   As there I saw my Lord ;
And still my joy knows no surcease,
   While waiting on His Word.
Through all these years I've walked with Him,
   And felt His Presence near ;
My eye of Faith has not grown dim
   And still to me He's dear.

My grateful heart with love o'erflows ;
   My all to Him I've given ;
And He alone my gladness knows ;
   My service is my Heaven.
And, now, to me to live is Christ :
   I'm one with Him in love ;
With Him I daily keep my tryst ;
   I'll reign with Him above.

TO DIE IS GAIN.

(PHIL. i. 21.)

" To die is gain !" How can it be ?
'Tis life we love ; in it we see
Our fulness.   'Tis a strange refrain :
" To die is gain !" " To die is gain !"

" To die is gain !" What means this word ?
" To die ?"   What gain can death afford ?
How can we make this matter plain :
This Gospel truth—" to die is gain ?"

This death is gain,—to die to sin ;
To die to all that's wrong within,—
To envy, hate, to words that pain :
In dying thus " to die " is gain.

To die to pride and all pretence ;
To die to that which gives offence ;
To uttered words that leave a stain
Upon our lips,—such death is gain.

To die to selfish, grasping greed ;
To all that shuts our hearts 'gainst need ;
To words unkind—of life the bane—
In all such death " to die " is gain.

To die to cold and callous heart;
To every act that leaves a smart;
To evil thoughts and all things vain :
To die to these is truly gain.

To die for men, as Jesus died ;
To suffer, ay, be crucified—
The Lamb of God for sinners slain—
In death like this " to die " is gain.

" To die " is not to cease to be;
In death the spirit is set free—
Free from the body's clogging chain—
And soars to Heav'n.   " To die *is* gain."

" To die " is to begin to live
The higher life which Christ doth give;
" To die " is to begin to reign
With Christ above.   Is *this* not gain ?

To dwell where all the holy meet,
In love and fellowship most sweet :
'Tis this to die—O sweet refrain :
" To die is gain "—" To die is gain."

THE NEW NAME.

"And I will write upon him My new name."—Rev. iii. 12.

"I'LL write upon him My New Name :"
My Lord, I would Thy promise claim ;
Thy "*New* Name "—'tis my heart's desire,—
O write it large in words of fire !

Thy "*New* Name !" who may understand
All that it means in glory land ?
Who, if he knew how much it meant,
Would pray to have such blessing sent ?

"Thy New Name "—do we ask this prize
With sealèd or half-opened eyes,—
Not knowing what we ask or crave,—
Or can we know this side the grave ?

Thy "New Name "—he who would it bear
Must also Thine own image wear ;
Must love all that which Thou dost love
On sin-cursed earth, in Heaven above.

I

He must, like Thee, all glory give
To God, the Father; he must live
In loving sympathy with men,
And strive to lead them home again.

He must be patient, gentle, meek,
His lips be pure, pure words to speak;
His life be true, his heart be brave;
His soul a-yearning souls to save.

All love of self he must o'ercome;
In praise of self he must be dumb;
No arrogance, pretence, or pride,
Must ever in his heart abide.

He must not set his heart on pelf;
His neighbour he must love as self;
To poor and needy he'll give food,
And aye find joy in doing good.

He'll yield himself a sacrifice
Alive to God; and in his eyes
No humble work will seem too small,
If God be glorified withal.

Those only who are freed from sin,
Can hope our Lord's " New Name " to win ;
To him who overcomes, 'tis said,
Will honour such as this be paid.

The holier and humbler we,
The higher—thus it seems to me—
Will be our joys and name and place :
In Heav'n reward is all of grace.

Before our world was cursed by sin ;
Before man's rebel will within
Had shattered all his princely power,
And spoiled him of his highest dower,

He had a language and the skill
To name the animals at will ;
According to its nature each
Was named and called in human speech.

So vast the intellect of man,
Till sin had placed it under ban,
That numbers, almost infinite,
Seemed but as nothing in his sight.

So in the Homeland there will be
A language full, expressive, free,
And skill to name and value each
By names adapted to Heav'n's speech.

There our " New Name " will indicate
Our worth, our measure, and our weight—
As known to Christ and the redeemed,—
Not as to earthly eye we seemed.

This our reward—our Lord's " New Name,"—
The brightest wreath in glory's fame,—
Whoever hears it knows our worth,
And knows the life that gave it birth.

Who would not, then, most faithful be,
And seek, Lord, to become like Thee ;
To perfect holiness lay claim,
And win the highest, best " New Name."

THE MOUNT OF HOLINESS.

O HOLY Mount where Jesus dwells!
  Thy heights are clear and bright;
With ardent love my bosom swells
    To bask in thy pure light.
I long to breathe the bracing air
    Of Holiness and Love;
I joy to know that man may dare
    To dwell with saints above.

The way at times seems long and steep,
    But help is ever nigh;
And all in the right path may keep,
    Who fix on Christ their eye.
Then higher, higher let us climb
    Up to the Mount of God,
Until we reach the topmost heights—
    The heights which Jesus trod.

What though with toil and weary tread
    We wend our upward way;
Each onward step will bring us near
    To Everlasting Day.
The joys of Earth we leave behind,
    For Christ is our desire;
No word inspires us like the call:
    "Come, let us go up higher."

BREAD OF HEAVEN.

"Then said they unto Him: Lord, evermore give us this bread."—St John vi. 34.

PART I.

"Lord, evermore give us this bread:"
　How grandly breathes this noble prayer!
How sweet to know men may be fed
　With Bread from Heaven—angels' fare.
　　"I am that Bread of Life," said He;
　　'Tis for those that believe in Me.

Lord, evermore give ME this Bread,—
　Give me Thyself, Thy Life, Thy Love;
As Thou for me hast lived and bled,
　And promised glorious life above;
　　Now feed me with this Bread of Heav'n—
　　Thyself, Thy Life—for mortals given.

Lord, evermore give me this Bread—
　Thy Flesh, Thy Blood, of souls the life;
For, Lord, all men by sin are dead,
　And soul and body are at strife;
　　And Thou alone true life canst give,
　　And bid dead souls anew to live.

PART II.

Lord, evermore give me this Bread:
I crave it for both heart and head,—
Food for the mind, the heart, the soul,—
This my desire, and this the whole:
 Not pleasure, luxury, or ease,
 Nor things that self and passion please.

Lord, evermore give me this Bread:
Of sinful thoughts fill me with dread,
My soul with holy longings fill;
Thy Love into my heart instil;
 O keep me near Thee day by day;
 In every trial be my stay.

Lord, evermore give me this Bread:
In Thine own footsteps I would tread;
With Bread of Heaven for my fare,
I shall be strong to do and dare;
 In lowly service follow Thee;
 While blest myself, a blessing be.

Lord, evermore give me this Bread:
I would by Thy good Hand be led;
O let me walk close by Thy side,
With Thy good Spirit for my Guide;
 In patience doing Thy sweet will,
 That Thine own fulness may me fill.

Lord, evermore give me this Bread :
Give Faith to grasp all Thou hast said ;
Give Love and Trust, that I may run
With Joy the race in Thee begun :
     My every thought and word inspire ;
     My lips touch Thou with Holy Fire.

Lord, evermore give me this Bread :
Thy Spirit's Pow'r upon me shed ;
In Pentecostal fulness shower
The riches of Thy gracious dower :
     Thus filled and quickened, I will be
     Glad willing messenger for Thee.

GOD'S LEADING.

"And He led them forth by the right way."—Psalm cvii. 7.

" He led them by the right way ; "
At first by night, and then by day ;
Again in darkness, then in light ;
In all His leading He led right :
     He led them into rest—
     A tribe supremely blest.

God's Leading.

From bondage sore in Egypt land,
He led them forth with mighty hand;
In love to them He spoiled their foes,
And plagued the king who 'gainst them rose
     He led them through the sea,
      And gave sweet liberty.

For those He loved on that great day,
He caused the sea to flee away;
Where proud waves rolled He oped a way,
And led them o'er in grand array,—
     The sea on either hand,
      Their feet stood on dry land.

Amid the dangers of the deep
They trusted God; He them did keep;
Presumptuous foes at them did rush;
Their frantic zeal He quick did hush,—
     He cooled it in the sea,
      And triumphed gloriously.

He loves them still; He loves no less;
But, lo! the way's the wilderness;
A weary march, and dreary days;
For, see! they're led in devious ways
     For forty weary years,
      Their path bedewed with tears.

In all their wand'rings RIGHT they're led
With Bread from Heav'n they're daily fed:
Then why their doubts and anxious fears?
And why such murmurings and tears?
　　Ah, they have rebel wills,—
　　Distrust their proud hearts fills.

A weary march of forty years;
A dreary life, all steeped in tears;
A life of sinning and repenting,
Of proud self-will and heart-relenting,
　　With Canaan's Rest at hand—
　　The promised " goodly land."

Lo! forty years of wasted life!
Lo! forty years of sin and strife.
Before on Jordan's banks they stand
With FAITH enough to win the land!—
　　A land all theirs by right,—
　　A land for years in sight.

In love He led them all the way;
From heat of sun, a Cloud by day;
In darkness, Fire to give them light;
In danger, kept them by His might.
　　He led them into Rest—
　　A tribe supremely blest.

"JESUS ONLY."

TUNE—"MORNING LIGHT."

IN early life my Saviour
   Had often sought my heart;
But, gay, and loving pleasure,
   I bade the Lord depart:
In tender love He led me,
   Although I knew it not;
With richest bounty fed me,
   Nor yet my Lord I sought.

In love He oft did send me
   Some messenger of death,
And then in love befriend me
   By giving back my breath:
And now I strove to serve Him;
   But sought in vain for peace,—
By living to DESERVE Him
   My sorrow did not cease.

But when the loving Jesus
 Said, " Sinner, LOOK and LIVE,"
I LOOKED and found most precious
 The truth—" I FREELY give : "
In seeking " Jesus only "
 At once I found the rest
Which all obtain, who humbly
 Recline on Jesus' breast.

And now, on Him reclining
 In every step I take,
My heart knows no repining—
 I'M KEPT FOR JESUS' SAKE.
Dear Lord, to Thee I've given
 My life and all that's mine,—
My only home is Heaven,—
 MY JESUS, I AM THINE.

I would be humble, holy,
 With faith and zeal and love
To live for " Jesus only "—
 To reign with Him above:
I'd seek no earthly glory—
 ALL GLORY, LORD, IS THINE—
I'd lift up " Jesus only ; "
 Lord, may this joy be mine !

THE CHRISTIAN LIFE.

" Hé will be our Guide even unto death."—Psalm xlviii. 14.

Tune—" Rutherford."

THE tide of life is ebbing;
 We have no portion here!
The passing years remind us
 Eternity draws near.
The past is all behind us,—
 Its toils, and cares, and pain:
Its loves, and joys, and triumphs
 Evermore remain.

The joys of earth are transient—
 Its pleasures and its fame—
But Heav'n, and Christ, and duty
 To us are still the same.
Thy glory and Thy beauty,
 O Christ, we've seen before;
May Thy sweet presence fill us
 Now and evermore.

With grateful hearts, our Father,
 Thy holy name we praise;
For Thou hast loved and led us
 Through many devious ways:

In bounty Thou hast fed us,
    And made our cup run o'er;
We praise Thee for Thy goodness—
    Praise and ask for more.

Our joys and sorrows, blended,
    Have made our lives more sweet;
Our loneliness and weakness
    Oft brought us to Thy feet.
O Saviour, may Thy meekness,
    And gentleness, and love
Be ours, till we, rejoicing,
    Reach our home above.

Till then we seek Thy guidance,
    Thy love and daily care,
To live in sweet communion
    With Thee by faith and prayer.
Make strong the bond of union
    That binds our hearts to Thee;
From sin may Thy good Spirit
    Make and keep us free.

O give us sweet submission
    To Thy most blessed will;
All hearts with sorrow riven
    With Thine own presence fill.

With Christ, and hope, and heaven,
  Our hearts shall know no fear;
For we shall feel Thy presence,
  Jesus, Saviour, near.

THREE VOICES.

TUNE—CHURCH PRAISE, No. 155.

OLD YEAR :—" Your days are swiftly passing,
      Your life is brief and frail."
    Thus speaks the dying Old Year
      With earnest solemn wail.
    It speaks of offers slighted,
      Of vows too lightly made,
    Of budding hopes all blighted,
      Of love too long delayed.

NEW YEAR :—" Rise up in all your manhood,
      Be true, and pure, and strong."
    Thus speaks the opening New Year.
      We usher in with song.
    O Jesus! we are sinful,
      We need Thy pard'ning love;
    Our strength is perfect weakness,
      O send help from above.

JESUS :—" Go ye into my Vineyard,
  And work, and watch, and pray."
O Jesus! make us faithful;
  Inspire us day by day;
Give zeal, and love of duty;
  Give faith, and peace, and power;
Reveal to us Thy beauty;
  Be Thou our strong high tower.

JESUS:—" My presence shall go with thee,
  And I will give thee rest."
Then, Jesus, we will claim Thee
  As our abiding Guest:
And Thou wilt be our comfort,
  Our Guide, our Strength, our Joy
And we, in Thy blest service,
  Will all our powers employ.

JESUS :—" And be ye also ready,
  The Bridegroom cometh soon."
Blest Jesus! we are watching
  All through the night's dark noon.
Our lamps are bright and burning;
  We're waiting for the King;
Our eyes are heavenward turning:
  What joy that day will bring!

CALL TO CONSECRATION.

TUNE—ARMAGEDDON.

WHO will COME to Jesus ?
  Who will come to-day—
Come for peace and pardon,
  Learn to watch and pray ?
Who will look to Jesus,
  Day by day, for grace,
Loving, hoping, trusting,
  Seeing His bright face ?
Saviour, I will seek Thee,
  Trust Thy love divine,
Look to Thee for keeping :
  I am ever Thine.

Who will WORK for Jesus—
  Work with heart and will—
Leading weary mortals
  Up to Zion's hill ?
Who will be a soldier
  In our Captain's band,
Marching, fighting, conquering,
  With strong heart and hand ?
                    K

Saviour, I will serve Thee
  In Thy cause divine—
Follow where Thou leadest :
  I am only Thine.

Who'll be ALL for Jesus,
  Strong to do and dare,
Faithful, true, and holy,
  Trusting to His care ?
Who'll submit with Jesus
  To the Father's will,
Hushing every murmur,
  Saying, " Peace, be still ? "
Saviour, I would follow
  In Thy steps divine ;
Lead me where Thou pleasest :
  I am wholly Thine.

Are you ready, Christian,—
  Ready for the King ;
Waiting for His welcome,
  For the robe and ring ?
Watch for His appearing ;
  Watch with joy and song ;
For His Spirit, cheering,
  Makes the heart grow strong.

Saviour, by Thy mercy,
  By Thy love divine,
I am always ready—
  Ever, only Thine.

CONSECRATION.

FATHER, our hearts inspire
  To worship Thee;
Fill us with fond desire
  Thy face to see.
While at Thy throne we gaze,
In songs of joy and praise
Our hearts in faith we raise,
  O Lord, to Thee.

Lord, in this solemn hour,
  Give us to see
Some tokens of Thy power
  And love so free.
Thy goodness we adore;
Thy mercy we implore;
Our hearts fill evermore
  With love to Thee.

Accept our humble vow
   To live for Thee:
Blest Spirit, fill us now,
   And make us free.
When self asserts its power,
When clouds of sorrow lower,
Our hearts bind in that hour
   Closer to Thee.

Our empty hearts we bring,
   On bended knee;
O fill us, as we cling
   By faith to Thee!
Come, Saviour, in Thy love,
Dwell in us, Heavenly Dove,
Till in our Home above
   We're safe with Thee.

SHINING FOR CHRIST.

Tune—Shine, Christian, Shine.

Shine 'mid the darkness, Christian;
Shine where the wild waves beat;
Shine in the early gloaming;
   Invite to a safe retreat:

Shine in the early morning;
Shine with the Sun's first ray;
Shine while the world is toiling,
    And light up the toiler's way.

CHORUS:

Shine! shine! shine! shine, Christian, shine;
See that your lamp is always bright;
Shine! shine! shine! shine, Christian, shine,
    Jesus Himself is thy light.

Say not, 'My light is feeble';
Say not, 'I cannot shine;
Trim well your light, my brother;
    For yours is a lamp divine:
Life is the lantern, sister,
Jesus Himself the light,
Keep then your lantern burnished,
    That Jesus may shine full bright.

See all those struggling seamen,
Dashing the wild waves' foam!
Hark! there's a cry in the darkness;
    Then light the poor wand'rer home:
Tell of the love of Jesus:
He is this dark world's light;
Tell it to the Father's glory,
    And praise Him both day and night.

NEW YEAR'S HYMN.

Tune—Dresden.

AGAIN the bells are ringing
　　In peals of joyous cheer;
Again we join to welcome
　　The bright and glad New Year.
O Father, deign to bless us,
　　And fill each heart with joy;
Reveal to us Thy presence;
　　Give peace without alloy.
　　　Make us more like Jesus,
　　　More gentle, loving, true;
To Thee our service and our life
　　We consecrate anew.

The past was full of blessing,
　　For Thou didst guide and keep;
And some were called to service,
　　While some were called to weep:
But by Thy hand upholding,
　　We trod the heav'nward way;
And Thy good Spirit, cheering,
　　Turned darkness into day.
　　　Bless us still, Lord Jesus;
　　　Our vows we now renew;

To Thee our service and our life
We consecrate anew.

The present is for service,
  For deeds of faith and love,
For helping weary mortals
  To reach the home above.
Lord Jesus, make us faithful,
  And clothe us all with power;
Bestow on us rich blessing—
  A Pentecostal shower.
    Day by day, Lord Jesus,
    Thy love we'll keep in view;
To Thee our service and our life
  We consecrate anew.

The future lies before us,
  In Jesus bright and clear;
With Christ and hope and heaven
  Our hearts shall know no fear.
Give faith, and joy, and power,
  That we may live for Thee,
Then, with the ransomed army,
  Thy face in glory see.
    Help us, blessed Jesus,
    To keep our Home in view,
While now our service and our life
  We consecrate anew.

NEW YEAR'S HYMN.

(Church Praise, No. 369.)

Another year for Jesus!
Lord, bless this year to me!
   Angels attending,
   From ill defending,
From sin O keep me free:
   Thy love and fear
Fill all the coming year.
Another year for Jesus,
Lord, bless this year to me!

Another year for Jesus!
Perchance a year of pain,
   Of lonely sorrow
   On each to-morrow;
But loss to me is gain:
   While Christ is mine
My heart shall ne'er repine.
Another year, etc.

Another year for Jesus!
Let service be my joy;
   Thy Spirit filling,
   Make my heart willing;

New Year's Hymn.

Give peace without alloy:
  Thy love and power
Attend me every hour.
Another year, etc.

Another year for Jesus!
Lord, make me more like Thee!
    I'd seek no glory,
    I'd tell the story
Of what Thou didst for me.
    My heart is blest,
For Thou hast given me rest.

Another year for Jesus!
The past I can't recall;
    I'd claim the present,
    And make it pleasant
By kindly deeds to all.
    Thy love and grace
Help me Thy steps to trace.

Another year for Jesus!
I'm nearer to my home;
    The light shines clearer,
    The rest is nearer,
My heart seeks less to roam.
    My heart is filled,
And by Thy Spirit stilled.

NEW YEAR'S HYMN.

Tune—"St. Gertrude."

Welcome, gladd'ning New Year,
　Bright with bells and song,
Glad with friendly greetings,
　Make us true and strong.
Jesus is our Leader
　In each step we take;
We'll march on rejoicing,—
　Kept for Jesus' sake.
　　"Looking unto Jesus"
　　　Makes the feeblest strong;
　　And His love and favour
　　　Fill the heart with song.

Keep us near Thee, Saviour,
　Through the coming year;
Walking in Thy footsteps,
　Naught have we to fear.
Thou hast been our Helper,
　Giving strength and peace,
Give us still Thy blessing—
　Joys that never cease.
　　"Looking unto Jesus"
　　　Will our watchword be;
　　Day by day Thou'lt keep us
　　　Clinging close to Thee.

New Year's Hymn.

Keep us "meek and lowly,"
　　Restful, cheerful, free;
Make us pure and holy,—
　　More and more like Thee.
Give us power in service,
　　Joy in doing good;
Make us prize Thy favour
　　More than daily food.
　　　"Looking unto Jesus"—
　　　　Words of precious power!
　　　They will be our comfort
　　　　Till our dying hour.

NEW YEAR'S HYMN.

TUNE—"ROCKINGHAM," or "COMMUNION."

WE thank and praise Thee, Saviour dear,
For all Thy mercies through the year;
For love, and peace, and blessing given;
For every help to lead to Heaven.

In looking o'er the past we trace
Thy guiding hand, Thy love, Thy grace;
With heavenly gifts our cup runs o'er;
We thank Thee, Lord, and ask for more.

We ask Thee for a lowly mind;
We ask for love to all mankind;
We ask for purity and power;
We ask Thy presence every hour.

We consecrate in this New Year,
Ourselves and all we hold most dear;
We would be faithful, loving, true,
And do whate'er Thou bidd'st us do.

Accept, O Lord, our solemn vow;
O bless each one, O bless us now!
In every step throughout this year
Help us to feel Thy presence near.

Whene'er we feel temptation's power;
In sorrow's darkest, saddest hour;
In weakness, sickness, doubt, and fear,
Be thou, good Spirit, ever near.

Meet with us in Thy House, we pray;
Be in the School each Sabbath day;
In every Home be Thou a Guest;
O bless us, and we shall be blest.

SELECTIONS FROM EARLY POEMS,

Written in College Days,

AND

PUBLISHED IN VARIOUS PERIODICALS

IN

NOVA SCOTIA, CANADA.

SELECTIONS FROM EARLY POEMS.

FOR AN ALBUM.

YOUTHFUL, buoyant, joyous, free,
Full of life and liberty,
    Thou art now ;
Naught of sorrow dost thou share,
Not the shadow of a care
    Shades thy brow.

Life ahead is all uncertain,
Never seek to lift the curtain
    Wisdom drew ;
But for each event the rather
Trust in God : the loving Father
    Cares for you.

He who makes the lilies grow,
Clothed in beauty pure as snow,
    Feeds His own :
They grope in night who will not trust ;
But, in love, for all the just
    " Light is sown."

"Bread of Heaven" be thy food!
Joy and peace and every good
    Here be thine!
Glory's crown be richly set,—
Studded like a coronet,—
    Stars that shine!

A SUMMER'S MORN.

Aurora's blush is on the sky,
The east is gilt with dawning day;
Before Morn's face the shadows fly,
Each star withholds its silver ray.

The anxious queen of night grows pale,
While Morn unlocks the gates of night;
And o'er her face she draws a veil
To hide her from Morn's gleaming light.

The modest stars retire from view—
Their silvery radiance curtain o'er—
That blushing Morn's bright rosy hue
May gild the edge of day the more.

The glorious sun, with vision bright,
Peeps thro' the golden gates of day;
His smile dispels the gloom of night,
And makes the face of Nature gay.

The rosy footsteps of the Morn
Now lightly tread on hill and dale;
While Sol's bright rays the hills adorn
And deck with gems the dewy vale.

The wakeful lark his matin trills,
And early greets the merry morn,
Ere Phœbus glads the cloud-capp'd hills,
Or Venus of his beams are shorn.

Glad Nature joins Morn's early song;
Her face assumes its brightest hue;
Responsive woods re-echo song,
With leafy locks still steep'd in dew.

Anon the genial king of day
Looks down on mother-earth's fair bowers
With loving eye and beaming ray,
To kiss the dew-tears from the flowers.

The blushing flow'rets lift their heads
And meekly ope their golden eyes;
Their wet glad face sweet fragrance sheds,
Which Morn's own rosy breath outvies.

All Nature now is bright and gay,
The voice of song is in the grove;
Each songster trills his morning lay,
To praise the God whom all should love.

L

Then why should man with thankless heart,
Refuse to swell the song of praise;
O mortal! fail not in thy part;
But, lark-like, let thy matins raise.

Then will the light of glory's morn
Dawn on thy soul with cheering ray;
The sun of glory will adorn
Thy brow with everlasting day.

THE TALKING ZEPHYR.

HARK! the evening Zephyr's stealing
    Its airy way into the bower;
List! its breezy hand is feeling,
    For the fairest, sweetest flower.

Zephyr, tell me why thou'rt creeping
    Softly 'mong the tiny flowers;
Why, when other winds are sleeping,
    Dost thou seek the garden bowers?

"I have come," replied the Zephyr,
    "To fan the flow'rets ere they fade—
Come for balm to breathe, as ever,
    On some toil-worn, aching head.

"I have come, too, as a vesper,
　Breathing sweetness in my song;
Come to tell thee in a whisper,
　Th' eve of life will come ere long.

"Balmy is my breath at even,
　Yet it sighs for parting day,
Weeping dew-tears like a pilgrim
　Saddened by the Sun's last ray.

"Therefore, hear my whisp'rings, mortals,
　Haste to speed you on your way;
Linger not lest Heaven's portals
　Close against you while you stay."

Welcome, balmy whispering Zephyr;
　Welcome, spirit-voice of even;
Welcome, dewy-breath that ever
　Wafts the soul in thought to Heaven.

I would learn of thee, sweet Zephyr,
　To gather balm for aching hearts;
I would say to mortals ever,
　"Time is fleeting—life departs."

THE TWO FLOWER GARDENS.

How richly decked the garden bower
   With beauty Nature lent it!
How sweet the fragrance of the flower
   With Nature's perfume scented!

Nor is the lovely garden-plot
   Merely a thing of beauty;
Those angel-flowers around the cot
   Whisper of love and duty.

Their voiceless tongues like angels speak,
   Breathing,—Truly, God is love,
Who made the Rose's smiling cheek
   Fair enough to bloom above.

Who made the Tulip's breath so sweet,
   That seraph-lips might taste it.
The loved Forget-me-not as neat
   As if His own smile graced it.

We also hear the call of duty
   From flower-entwinèd bowers,
Which whisper, "While you praise our beauty,
   Thank God who made the flowers."

God's hand alone has deck'd the flowers
  With golden sunset blushes;
He feeds them with His dewy showers,
  His sun their pure cheeks flushes.

There is another precious bower,
  The garden of the mind,
Where Virtue's buds and Love's sweet flowers
  A genial soil may find.

There Purity's sweet budding bowers,
  When sunned by Virtue's rays,
Expand in meekly-blushing flowers
  Of worth and happiness.

The Daisy's innocence when twined
  With myrtle leaves of Love,
And Lily-buds, with these combined,
  Give bowers like those above.

O'er bowers decked with Faith's bright flowers,
  Hope's buds breathe sweet perfume;
When sorrow's storm-cloud o'er it lowers,
  Love's rays dispel the gloom.

This garden bower has many a flower
  That all should fondly cherish;
For Virtue's bowers of blushing flowers,
  Neglected, quickly perish.

These flowerets fair, so pure and rare,—
These lovely, Christian graces—
That bud below, perennial grow,
And bloom in heavenly places.

A MIDMIGHT REVERIE.

OFT, as twilight draws the curtain
O'er the fleeting, dull, uncertain
   Labours of the weary day,
Calliopé,—voice of beauty,—
On her round of Epic duty,
   Breathes into my soul a lay,—
Fitful, quick, impatient, pressing,
Not like other "fair"—*caressing*,—
   Breathes upon my soul of clay.

Why content thyself with plodding,
Digging, diving, often nodding
   O'er the rusty, musty lore
Of the treatise theologic,
Of the puzzling paragogic
   Letters in the page of yore?
Poesy betimes will cheer thee,
Love and Beauty still be near thee,
   Ev'n as in the days of yore.

Come! a truce to story's pages!
Let Oblivion keep those ages,
  That have fall'n o'er mem'ry's brink!
Create anew : with thought all glowing
Cull fair flowers, new life bestowing;
  Fancy still to Fancy link ;
Let freshest " births of intellect "
Grace a page you oft have decked,
  While at Musa's fount you drink.

Not like balmy whispering zephyr,
Not like spirit-voice, that ever
  Whispers softly in the ear,
Comes the gush from Musa's fountain :
Like the rush adown the mountain
Of the limpid plashing waters,—
Playful, dancing Naiad's daughters,—
  Impatient Musa doth appear,
Bounding, rushing, rolling ever,
Swelling, gushing, halting never,
  Except perchance to spy a tear.

Pensive oft, and melancholic,
Often full of fun and frolic
  Was Apollo's tuneful lyre ;
Joy-inspiring, care-forgetting,
Passion-firing, then regretting,
  Is the glow of Bacchus' fire :

But the Muse, impelled by duty,
Sings of Fame, and Love, and Beauty,
Fills the heart with pure emotion,
Gently, and without commotion,
    Lifts the spirit higher.

SOLITUDE.

I.

ALONE! alone in a lonely world!
    Away from the home of my youth!
My barque heavy-laden, my canvas all furled,
Now toss'd by the gale, now skyward hurled,
    No friend—no Naomi, like Ruth.
One comfort I have, one solace in woe,
One silvery ray, wherever I go,—
    My piety, virtue, and truth.

II.

Alone! alone! no spirit akin!
    No loved one to cherish and bless!
No part in the world, 'mid its bustle and din!
No smile from without—no joy from within—
    No helpless to aid in distress:
Who can feel this is life, or say it is good,
Thus in Solitude's chamber ourselves to seclude,
    As if there were naught to possess?

III.

Alone ? Ah, no ; I am not alone ;
  There are friends on the sunny shore,
Whose voices are heard, with their rich mellow
    tone,
Whose bounties each day are most lavishly
    strown—
  To fail me, I trust, nevermore.
Who would be alone, with solitude wed ;
With Despair's bitter herbs content to be fed ?
  Not I ; my solitude's o'er.

IV.

'Tis sweet to have basked in the sunny light
  Of a friend I had loved before ;
To have ris'n in the power of my manhood's
    might,
Above the dark clouds that bedimmed delight,
  To banish distrust evermore.
O Friendship, thou gem of the richest hue,
Be mine for aye, and be ever true,
  Till we "meet to part no more."

LOVE'S TOKEN.

I.

May I not say, 'I love thee,'—
I who have felt the power
Of that pure deep emotion
For many a precious hour ?
I prize thee as a treasure,
A gem of purest ray,
A source of ceaseless pleasure—
The sweetest flower of May.

II.

E'er would I say, 'I love thee':
To me thou art most dear;
For oft thy tongue's sweet melody
Has charmed my ravished ear.
I hear thee as a whisper
Of love from heaven above,
Or as a heavenly vesper,
Breathed in sweet tones of love.

III.

I hear thee, yes, I hear thee,
In the purling of the rill,
Whose waters dance so nimbly
To the wild-bird's song so shrill;
I hear thee in the music
Breathed by the forest choir,
In every strain that issues
Forth from the Muse's lyre.

IV.

In each sweet sound I hear thee—
In chimes of Sabbath bells,
In every voice that calls me
To where my Saviour dwells.
I hear thee in the zephyr,
That soothes the mind at even ;
In spirit-voice that ever
Speaks to the heart of heaven.

V.

In every flower I see thee,
That's pure, and sweet, and rare,
In purest, meek-eyed daisy
Thy gentle eye is there.
I see thee in the bower
With sweetest roses twined ;
The little blue-eyed flower
Thee quickly calls to mind.

VI.

In rainbow-tints I see thee ;
In golden clouds at even—
In everything where beauty
Inspires a thought of Heaven.
I see thee in the rosy hues
That gild the early morn,
And in the drops of sparkling dews
That gem both rose and thorn.

VII.

I see thee, yes, I see thee
In the radiant queen of night,
In the beams she sheds so gently
In pure and pearly light.
I see thee in the star-lit sky—
In those bright eyes of night,
That beam so soft and lovingly,
Like thine own eyes so bright.

VIII.

A morning-star I see thee
Whose praises poets hymn,
Still glowing in the *social* skies
When lesser lights are dim.
I see thee, too, in dream-land
By bright-eyed Fancy's aid,
While wand'ring by some streamlet
Or roaming wooded glade.

IX.

By Faith's quick eye I see thee,
As, when on bended knee,
Devotion, pure and holy,
Breathes a fond prayer for thee.
And may I ever see thee,
A bright and sparkling gem,
In Jesus' blood washed throughly—
Set in His diadem.

FORGET ME NOT.

(Sent with a posy of FORGET-ME-NOTS.*)*

WHEN on this wreath of Love's own flowers,
You cast a glance in lonely hours ;
May voiceless tongues—O tender thought !
Then gently breathe—" Forget me not."

When Mem'ry muses on these lines,
And Friendship's sun most brightly shines ;
Then rest assured a friend you've got,
Who also breathes—" Forget me not."

Thy worth I prize—thy face so fair ;
For Virtue sits divinely there :
Thine eye, with love so richly fraught,
E'er gently speaks—" Forget me not."

Sweet flowers of Faith's unchanging hue ;
Dear types of Love and Friendship true ;
Breathe forth fond words—words ne'er forgot—
And say for me—" Forget me not."

ODE TO SPRING.

I.

When sovereign Winter, tired of sway,
　His icy sceptre lays aside,
To northern climes he hies away,
　There with cold Boreas to reside;
For sunny realms delight him not,
Nor verdant bowers, nor shady grot.

II.

Then gentle Spring steps forth with grace,
　With balmy zephyrs in her hands;
And fans dame Nature's pallid face—
　Afflicted sore with icy bands:
For Spring is genial, kind, and fair,
And ever breathes a balmy air.

III.

She Nature robes in living green,
　And brings sweet warblers to the grove;
Bright flowers and opening buds are seen;
　Which all proclaim a reign of love:
For Springtime its sweet beauty owes
To Him from Whom all Beauty flows.

MY BIRTHDAY.

My birthday! has it come again?
How quickly pass the rapid years!
In sober birthdays I would fain
Rejoice, yet mingle joy with tears.

Reflection, looking o'er the past,
Recalls bright scenes and happy hours,
Which pleasant seem'd and long did last,
As if life's path were strewn with flowers.

My merry school-boy days, how glad!
When books and play alike gave joy;
When thoughtful mood ne'er made me sad,
Nor care depressed the merry boy.

And e'en when boyhood yielded up
Its pleasures to more sober cheer,
Then, too, o'erflowed fond pleasure's cup,
And poured down bounties all the year.

But yet there is a darker shade,
However bright the picture's drawn,
Resolves forgot,—desires obeyed,—
And wayward youth still gliding on.

How many careless hours were spent,
Which study might have made to yield
A bounteous harvest, and have lent
A charm to life—'gainst sin a shield !

How little done for other's aid,
Beyond the circle of my home !
How oft from duty's pathway strayed
In pleasure's flowery fields to roam !

Methinks were I again to run
Life's race from early morn till now,
I would not do all I have done—
Would earlier to religion bow.

Could I life's pathway now retrace,
With skill to know what weeds have grown
From seeds, which wayward youth did place,
Among the seeds of virtue sown,

I fear for every grateful flower
I'd find to deck the pathway's side,
Full many a bitter weed would tower,
Refusing its bold face to hide.

But yet there are some fragrant flowers
Of lovely tint and gentle hue ;
For love's sweet buds and friendship's bowers
Bloomed sweetly, wet with heaven's dew.

Hence, while I'd mourn o'er follies past,
And fain would much from mem'ry blot,
Were I anew my life to cast
I would retain one sunny spot.

The loves and friendships of my youth
I would not wish now to efface ;
My love of home, of God, of Truth,
I could not now with aught replace.

And may each future birthday find
Life's pathway strewn with fairer flowers—
A truer heart—a richer mind—
More meetness for the heavenly bowers.

THE MISSIONARY.

O BRAVE, devoted man of God
  Whose heart for souls doth yearn—
Souls that in error's paths have trod
  Nor our God's laws could learn.

Around thee now with tearful eye
  We wreaths of fond loves twine,
As thou from all that's dear dost hie,
  From our sweet home and thine.

O sorrow-stricken one! for thee
　　Our sympathies outflow,
That in thy hand thy life will be
　　While toiling here below.

We sigh that thou thy life must spend
　　In some lone barbarous clime;
And die far off from earthly friend,
　　Perchance before thy time.

Ten thousand prayers for thee ascend
　　Up to the throne of grace,
That God would cause stout hearts to bend
　　Before thy heaven-lit face.

Thou hast with thee a mighty power—
　　The Word of God most pure,—
A cordial in life's saddest hour,
　　An anchor safe and sure.

No carnal weapon dost thou crave
　　Thy person to defend;
No band of warriors, strong and brave,
　　To thee their aid doth lend.

Yet, Heaven-born man, thou marchest on
　　Without dismay or dread;
For souls immortal must be won
　　To Christ thy glorious Head.

The thought that thou a soul may'st save
  From bitter endless woe,
Doth nerve thy noble soul to brave
  The sea, the sword, the foe.

Thy trust is not in strength of arms
  Or manly bravery,
But in Him who each foe disarms
  That wishes ill to thee.

Thine armour is thy trust in God,
  And in His promise sure;
Thy weapon is His Holy Word—
  The Word of truth most pure.

A glorious warfare thou dost wage
  'Gainst Satan's earth-born band;
The powers of hell thou dost engage—
  They fall before thy hand.

O noble one—a conqueror now—
  How generous to the foe!
Thou only seekest when and how
  Thou love to him may'st show.

A joy thou dost to him impart;
  A peace thou dost bestow,
Which flows but from a pardoned heart,
  That's freed from guilt and woe.

THE ILL-FATED "ATLANTIC."

(Wrecked near Halifax, N.S., April 1st, 1873.

Ten hundred souls—a precious freight!
A gallant ship, and a crew to mate
    Are hurled on a rugged shore;
No wistful look, nor bated breath,—
No thought of harm, nor dream of death—
    Betokens the breakers' roar.

'Tis a darksome night! all is peace within
Nor weltering wave, nor danger's din
    Disturbs the quiet slumber;
With a formal prayer in a hurried breath—
"Good Lord, deliver from sudden death,"—
    Lay down not a few of that number.

The mother has kissed her fond babe "good night;"
Her loving caress has disarmed affright,
    And the innocent sinks to rest,
Dreaming of toys, so rich and so rare—
Playthings and playmates—castles in air—
    And awakes—in the land of the blest.

Mothers and babes, no help do they crave;
Is there no one, *no one*, NO ONE to save
  The helpless, the loving, the fair ?
There's an earnest heart, and a willing hand;
But the frowning wave denies them the land,—
  They perish by hundreds there.

Husband and wife—"for better, *for worse*,"
Mother and child, nursling and nurse,
  Now prove the power of love :
Say now, "*Is love not stronger than death ?*"
Blest union ! unsevered while yet there is breath,
  'Twill consummate in Heaven above.

Ah, ill-fated ship, to destruction driven;
How many fond hearts are with anguish riven
  By thy dread and sudden disaster !
What homes have been ravaged, what loves have been
  buried,
How many true hearts to distraction were hurried
  That night by a *sleeping " master."*

From Swedish shores and Vaterland,
From Erin's homes and Angleland,
  Were snatched thy helpless prey ;
The promise of a friendly shore
Was broken, 'mid the breakers' roar,
  On All Fools' Day.

There were many who sought a home in the West—
There were some who reached the home of the blest,
    And a few a friendly shore;
Brave hearts nor woman nor child could save,
But ALL were engulfed in the angry wave—
    They sank to rise no more.

There were heroes there of no common hue,
Brady and Speakman, and Owens, too,
    And the "Ancient" mariner;
Long live these brave heroes—the great ones of earth,
May their mem'ry be fresh in the land of their birth,
    And in glory live forever.

MY SCHOOL.

Recited on retiring from the Headmastership of Guysborough
County Academy, Nova Scotia.

As I hie to my school in the morning,
    And look round on each face full of glee;
There's a voice,—a whisper of warning,—
    Speaking tenderly, softly to me:—
"O guard well those treasures of heaven,
    Whom God has intrusted to thee;
Imbue their young minds with the leaven
    Of truth, and a knowledge of ME."

While I gaze, with composure and pleasure
  On each face so frank and so free,
I fondly think each one's a treasure
  To father, and mother, and me.
I love to read history unwritten,
  As stamped on each bright budding mind;
And think of a future—though hidden—
  For each one that's good in its kind.

This eye is so bright and so beaming;
  That brow so noble and pure;
This face with such radiance gleaming:
  That countenance never demure;
This eye is so furtively glancing;
  That brow so sobered with thought;
On this cheek joy's dimples are dancing;
  None with sadness or sorrow is fraught.

Betimes, I sit dreamily thinking
  Of those young hearts unshadowed by care;
And while Fancy to Fancy I'm linking,
  I tenderly breathe a fond prayer;—
That the hearts of those dear ones may never
  Be blighted by sorrow or sin;
That the sweetness of Heaven may ever
  Be their sweetness and gladness within.

I gaze with fond pride on those faces,
　　That glow with delight while I teach;
And I fancy no nymph wore such graces,
　　As grace the fair features of each.
My heart-strings oft thrill with emotions
　　Of tenderest, watchfulest care,
As I think of the cares and commotions
　　That some of my dear ones must bear.

And betimes my heart yields—for 'tis human—
　　And the pulse of the future beats slow;
And, like sorrow in heart of a woman,
　　'Twill seek thro' my "sight" its outflow;
For I fear lest the tempter may find them,
　　And beguile some sweet innocent heart;
And if Vice with his shackles should bind them,
　　Oh! 'twould send thro' my vitals a dart.

Then I strive with more ardour than ever
　　To teach all that's lovely and pure;
That the sweetness of knowledge may never
　　Be embittered with thoughts that allure.
I seek to make study a pleasure,
　　As inviting as ball or croquet;
And it fills me with joy above measure,
　　That they're happy at books and at play.

The young mind is so easily moulded,
  Like the twig in the forest or field,
That its buds must with care be unfolded,
  Lest nor flower nor fruit it will yield.
It must not be ruthlessly bended;
  Therefore banish the rod and the rule;
Let love with instruction be blended,
  And affection will govern the school.

I think of those dear young immortals
  As buds on the family tree,
Which shall proudly o'ershadow the portals
  Of the mansions of bless yet to be.
Oh, how I have missed those sweet faces,
  Whose smiles wore a halo of light;
Who have gone with their sunshine and graces,
  To fill other hearts with delight.

And now I must leave these fair bowers;
  Nor hear the proud gush of their glee;
Nor receive their love-tokens in flowers,
  As they daily have brought them to me.
I shall miss them, oh, yes, I shall miss them—
  Those flowers from the garden of love;
But I'll pray that "Our Father" may bless them,
  And transplant them to His bowers above.

I trust I have faithfully tended,
   And cultured, and trained each fair flower;
For, while pruning and planting were blended,
   'Twas affection that reigned in this bower.
'Tis pleasant, when labour is ended,
   To think of the oft-honoured name
Of all who successfully wended
   Their way up the stern steeps of fame.

Thanks, then, to those hearts, young and tender;
   They have made me more noble and kind:
May their motto e'er be, " No surrender,"
   Till enriched by the triumphs of mind;
And while onward and upward they're pressing,
   With " Excelsior " stamped on their brow;
May angels stoop down with a blessing,
   While to God they submissively bow.

THE MINSTREL'S FATHERLAND.

(Translated from the German.)

WHERE is the Minstrel's Fatherland ?—
   Where sparks of noble spirits flew;
   Where flowers for Beauty's garland grew ;
   Where joyous hearts with vigour glowed ;
   Where love for all that's sacred flowed :
There was my Fatherland.

How NAMED—the Minstrel's Fatherland ?—
    It mourns sons slain by tyrant's hand ;
    And now it groans 'neath foreign strokes,
    Tho' once 'twas called the Land of Oaks,—
    THE FREE LAND ! THE GERMAN LAND !
Thus is named my Fatherland.

On WHOM CALLS thy Fatherland ?—
    It calls on Pity,—dumb with wonder,—
    With desperation's voice of thunder ;
    On Liberty to free the land ;
    On Retribution's vengeful hand :
On these calls my Fatherland.

Why WEEPS the Minstrel's Fatherland ?
    That tyrants' thunder it doth shake ;
    That sovereigns make the people quake ;
    That sacred promises are spurned ;
    And that its cry aside is turned :
Therefore weeps my Fatherland.

What WOULD the Minstrel's Fatherland ?
    It would remove all servile thrall ;
    The blood-hound chase from palace-hall ;
    And plant proud sons on freedom's land,
    Or *bed* them free beneath the sand :
This would my Fatherland.

What TRUSTS the Minstrel's Fatherland?
    It trusts in its most righteous cause;
    In people true to freedom's laws;
    And hopes for vengeance from above;
    For swift will come avenging Jove:
Thus hopes my Fatherland.

There is the Minstrel's Fatherland;
    There sparks of noble spirits flew;
    There flowers for Beauty's garland grew;
    There joyous hearts with vigour glowed;
    There love for all that's sacred flowed;
There is my Fatherland.

LIEUTENANT-GOVERNOR HOWE.

IN MEMORIAM.

Died at Halifax, June 1st, 1873.

TO-DAY we have laid him beneath the sod,
    The statesman, orator, bard—
His dust lies with dust, and his spirit's with God—
So pure and so noble was the path that he trod,
    That well did he merit reward.

He is gone! He lies honoured in the land of his
      choice,
  In the land of his love and his birth;
His promotion made hundreds of thousands rejoice;
His decease, alas! turns to mourning each voice—
  To-day there is *no* song of mirth.

The Tidings have spread o'er the land like a pall;
  The pulse of the nation is hushed;
The pride of our country, the idol of all,
So honoured in life, how resigned at the call
  That frail humanity crushed!

How composed is each line on the face of the dead!
  How serene the familiar brow!
How softly sealed is the eye that had shed
Such a radiant lustre, as the orator pled
  For the people,—the pen and the plough!

The highest in honour, the greatest in fame,
  Of her nobles, the dearest son,
The land of the Mayflower will cherish his name,
Ever bidding her children his virtues proclaim,
  And seek the proud place he had won.

He toiled for his country as no other toiled;
  His life was bound up in her weal;

When flushed with her honours, his hands were not soiled
    By ill-gotten gain; nor his country despoiled
      To reward "Joe Howe" for his leal.

We sadly and solemnly followed the bier,—
      While the minute-guns were firing,—
Full twenty thousand, who held him most dear,
With sorrowing words and a trickling tear,
      Which naught but love was inspiring.

All hearts and all flags were "half-mast high"
      For New Scotia's darling son;
Not the circle of kin alone heaved a sigh,
But the million has sorrowed with tear-bedewed eye
      That his course was so quickly run.

We all could have wished that our patriot's day
      Had been lengthened in honour and ease;
But "Our Father" had called the vet'ran away,—
When the summons comes, 'tis ours to obey,—
      He can take His own if He please.

IN MEMORIAM.

CLOUDS AND SUNSHINE.

(On the Death of a Fellow-Student.)

O FATHER! Thou hast called him home!
  The mother's hope—the sister's love!
His spirit hears the message—" Come,
  Come to realms of light above."

A cloud had settled on that brow;
  Betimes there dawned a gleam of light;
How sweet a thought for lov'd ones now,
  That Faith and Love then glowed so bright!

When naught of earth, or earthly joys,
  Can light the lamp that erst had shown,
A Saviour's love—a sister's voice—
  Brings truant reason to its throne.

No clouds bedim the vision now,—
  The messenger's a welcome guest;
For joy lights up the anguished brow
  Of him for whom " remains a rest."

He yields it up—this fitful life—
　Submissive to his Father's will;
No murmur speaks of inward strife,
　For Jesus whispers, " Peace, be still."

We loved him in our youthful days,—
　So noble, generous, and kind ;
We all bestowed our meed of praise—
　A tribute to his lofty mind.

We hoped to hear his lips proclaim
　The glorious Gospel of our Lord ;
But him Our Father did ordain
　A silent witness of " the Word."

We gaze upon the tranquil face,
　Th' unfurrowed brow, the sealèd eye,
The sweet familiar look we trace—
　Not here !—'tis there beyond the sky !

The lov'd is ta'en ; a blessing's left ;
　Faith, through her tears, lifts up the eye :
" Our Father, we are not bereft ;
　Our dear departed lives on high."

We are resigned ; he reigns above ;—
　Thou gav'st in love, in love didst take ;
And in the sunlight of that love
　We'll ever bask for Jesus' sake.

ON THE DEATH OF A CHILD.

(A Favourite Pupil.)

SWEET child! thou art gone from the home of thy
    birth,
  And sad thy departure has left us;
Thy dear sister Mary has ceased from her mirth
  Since God has of Tina bereft us.

Fond darling! no more wilt thou grace the proud knee
  Of thy grandsire who loved thee so dearly;
Nor wilt thou lisp "Dada" in tones of high glee,
  Which at all times made papa look cheerly.

No more wilt thou kiss sister Mary "good night,"
  Nor receive her fond love and caressing;
O 'tis hard to have parted such angels of light!
  But on each, we would hope, rests a blessing.

Sweet child! thou art gone to thy home in the skies,
  Heaven's choirs no longer could want thee;
On seraph's light wing thou must early uprise
  That God in His garden might plant thee.

N

HYMN ON AFFLICTION.

(Sent to a Fellow-Student during severe illness.)

AFFLICTED one, a Friend thou hast
    That closer than a brother clings;
Thy many cares upon Him cast;
    'Tis sweet relief that Jesus brings.

Why thy frail barque is toss'd—distress'd,
    And scarce can brave life's stormy sea,
Jesus can calm thy troubled breast,
    As once the waves of Galilee.

A lesson learn from Peter's faith,
    And firmly trust though billows roll;
" Be of good cheer," our Saviour saith,
    Through Me " thy faith shall make thee whole."

Then, wherefore should we fret and sigh,
    When by Affliction's stroke we're riven;
Nay, let us raise our thoughts on high,
    And look for bliss alone in Heaven.

Then, let all soldiers of the cross,
    Who feel a Father's chast'ning rod,
Still count all earthly joys but dross,
    And day by day grow liker God.

THE DYING YEAR.

THE passing year, so brief, so fleet,
  Has winged its flight how fast!
To all it speaks in accents meet,
  As it is flitting past:

"Thus to an end your days must come,
  However bright and fair;
Then, while thy course is being run,
  To meet thy God prepare.

"'Tis but a few short months since I
  Began my brief career;
But now I sicken—now I die:
  To you death may be near.

"But while the icy blast of death
  Is chilling every vein,
There comes a soul-reviving breath,
  Restoring life again.

"Thus, too, when your life-race is run,
  And death has sealed the eye,
Another life must be begun,
  For mortals never die."

TO THE SNOWDROP.

I.

LIKE bright and pearly dew-drop
　　On fragrant grass on Summer morn,
Art thou, pure, pretty Snowdrop,
　　Of Flora's daughters the first-born.

II.

Thou—fairest, dearest gift of Spring—
　　Art lovely in thy robes of white;
And, though thou'rt but a tiny thing,
　　To all thou givest pure delight.

III.

Thy drooping head and bashful face
　　Remind us of the modest maiden,
Who never seeks th' admirer's gaze,
　　Though with fair Virtue's flowers laden.

IV.

We gladly welcome thee, fair gem—
　　A sweet bright gleam of consolation—
First star in Flora's diadem,
　　As thou'rt first gem of vegetation.

Works by the Same Author.

THE GOSPEL IN GREAT BRITAIN—From St Patrick to John Knox and John Wesley.
Second Edition in the Press. Octavo, 340 pages, post free 3/9.

"A really valuable contribution to religious literature."—*Christian Commonwealth.*

"Admirable lectures, terse and telling. Rich in history, and as rich in instruction and warning. We very heartily commend the book."—*Evangelical Magazine.*

DOCTRINE AND DOUBT ; or, Christ the Centre of Christianity. *380 Octavo pages, post free 3/9.*

"This book is written by a 'Master of Assemblies.'"—*The Christian.*

"An able and earnest volume."—*Evangelical Magazine.*

"A most stimulating volume."—*Methodist Times.*

"Thoughtfully written for thoughtful people."—*Literary Churchman.*

"All through the book has the stamp of earnestness, thoughtfulness, and reality."—*Irish Ecclesiastical Gazette.*

JOY IN JESUS: Memorials of Bella Darling.
Cloth, 1/6, Morocco Gilt, 3/9. Stereotyped edition. 11th Thousand.

"This interesting biography of a charming young lady . . . . is an admirable book to give to any young ladies to lead them to Christ."—*The Christian Herald.*

"Well fitted at once to stimulate and guide young disciples to works of faith and labours of love."—*United Presbyterian Magazine.*

OUR CHILDREN FOR CHRIST---a full discussion of Baptism, with every text on the subject treated. *100 pages, cloth 9d. Third Edition. Post free.*

"Most conclusive and forcible, both in argument and scholarship."—*Horatius Bonar, D.D.*

"The book is one of marked ability, in our opinion irresistible."—*Christian News.*

THE WINES OF SCRIPTURE : or, Total Abstinence the True Temperance—a Biblical and Historical Inquiry. *Revised Edition. 4th Thousand. Cloth 6d., sewed 3d.*

"A singularly clear, terse, telling little treatise."—*The Outlook.*

"A capital contribution to the literature on the Wine question."—*Social Reformer.*

The Duty of the Christian Church in Relation to Temperance, (*Grand Division Prize Essay. The Property of the Grand Division of the Sons of Temperance, Nova Scotia*). *Third Thousand.*

THE BLESSED DEAD. *Sewed 3d. Only a few copies left.*

The Happy Life (*Third Edition*) and other works not enumerated above are out of print.